New Testament
Commentary Survey

NEW TESTAMENT
COMMENTARY SURVEY

Sixth Edition

D. A. CARSON

Baker Academic
Grand Rapids, Michigan

© 1986 1996, 2001, 2007 by D. A. Carson

Published by Baker Academic
a division of Baker Publishing Group
P.O. Box 6287, Grand Rapids, MI 49516-6287
www.bakeracademic.com

Printed in the United States of America

Library of Congress Cataloging-in-Publication Data

Carson, D. A.
    New Testament commentary survey / D. A. Carson. — 6th ed.
        p. cm.
    Includes bibliographical references and index.
    ISBN 10: 0-8010-3124-9 (pbk.)
    ISBN 978-0-8010-3124-3 (pbk.)
    1. Bible. N.T.—Commentaries—History and criticism. 2. Bible. N.T.—Commentaries—Bibliograhy. I. Title.
BS2341.2.C33 2007
016.2257—dc22   2006025659

Contents

PREFACE

In its first edition, this little book was written by Dr. (now Prof.) Anthony C. Thiselton and appeared under the title *Personal Suggestions about a Minister's Library*. In 1973, it was revised, and shortly after that the "Best Buys" section was brought up to date. That revision also introduced the change in title and format: *New Testament Commentary Survey* was born, the NT analogue of *Old Testament Commentary Survey* (both published, at the time, exclusively by British Theological Students' Fellowship). In 1976, I brought the book up to date again simply by adding additional paragraphs and by inserting new prices and publishing information where relevant. Apart from such modifications, Dr. Thiselton's comments were left unchanged. In 1984, the Theological Students' Fellowship asked for another revision, and this time it was thought unwise simply to add a few more paragraphs. It seemed more sensible to recast the entire work and enter it on a computer so that subsequent revisions, including price changes and the like, could be accomplished with less work than would otherwise be the case. With Professor Thiselton's kind permission, his text was sometimes incorporated into that third revision—occasionally with changes, especially on those rare occasions where I found myself mildly disagreeing with his assessment of a book. In the United States, Baker brought out the third edition. The fourth edition of this book appeared in 1993, and the fifth in 2001.

The years fly by, and new commentaries keep appearing—and so we have arrived at the sixth edition. Much of the checking was undertaken by one of my doctoral students, Jonathan Davis, to whom I owe an enormous debt.

The purpose of this short book is to provide theological students and ministers with a handy survey of the resources, especially commentaries, that are available in English to facilitate an understanding of the NT. The mature scholar is not in view. On the other hand, commentaries that are written at the popular level are generally given less attention than more substantive works. Theologically I am an evangelical, but many of the positive assessments offered in these notes are in connection with books written from the vantage point of some other theological tradition: the usefulness of a commentary sometimes turns on something other than the theological stance of its author—assuming, of course, that commentaries are read critically, as they should be whatever one's theological heritage. Conversely, just because a commentary stands within the evangelical tradition does not necessarily mean it is a good book. It may be thoroughly orthodox but poorly written, uninformed, or quick to import from other biblical passages meanings that cannot rightly be found in the texts on which comment is being offered. In other words, this *Survey* is a guide to commentaries, not orthodoxy. Nevertheless, I have not hesitated on occasion to draw attention to the theological "slant" of particular works. Such information is often as useful as comments on the work's level, general competence, and so forth. The restriction to English works is not absolute: occasionally I have included a foreign language work where nothing of a similar nature or stature exists in English. If I have not included more of them, it is because of my envisaged readership.

Prices and other publication data are, I hope, reasonably accurate and more or less comprehensive up to about the beginning of 2006, occasionally a bit beyond. At one time, book prices were more stable than they are now. Moreover, one used to be able to consult the latest edition of, say, *British Books in Print* to obtain current price information. But this work is no longer published, and online equivalents change prices so fast that they are not particularly useful as a guide to prices, especially on the British side. So the stipulation of, say, only an American price does not necessarily mean (as it did in earlier editions) that the work is not published on the British side. Moreover, nowadays readers anywhere in the world can purchase the same books through Internet companies, whose prices (less shipping) are usually way below list. So price information must now be read with more discretion than in earlier editions. I make no warranty of the accuracy of the information, both because the details change constantly and because almost certainly I have made some mistakes. On both sides of the Atlantic, it is often possible to beat the prices quoted here by purchasing from discount houses, special sales, or dot-com companies.

Related to changes in editions of commentaries, one must constantly examine what a new "edition" means. During the early 1980s, many of the TNTC and NCB volumes came out in new paperback editions, therefore boasting a new date even though all that had changed was the cover: the text was that of work done ten or twenty or more years earlier. The latest TNTC editions, however, are either work updated by the same author or commentaries by new authors replacing the earlier contributors.

Those interested in keeping up with the endless stream of commentaries need to consult the book review sections of journals. *The Expository Times* used to be first off the mark, but no longer, and an increasing number of its reviews are frankly eccentric. Reviews that usually keep the theological student in mind, and that are written from an evangelical perspective, are found in *Themelios*, whose quality has risen rapidly during the last few years. More comprehensive are the *Journal of Biblical Literature* and the *Catholic Biblical Quarterly*. Evangelical journals with useful reviews include (in addition to *Themelios*) *Churchman*, *Journal of the Evangelical Theological Society*, *Trinity Journal*, and *Westminster Theological Journal*. Older commentaries are treated to entertaining and sometimes profound comment in C. H. Spurgeon, *Commenting and Commentaries*, occasionally republished by Banner of Truth.

I have tried to scan the reviews of the fifth edition of this book and learn from them. On some matters I remain unrepentant. If I do not devote more space to United Bible Societies productions, for instance, it is because many of their commentaries, though doubtless of value to Bible translators, are of minimal use to theological students and ministers. One reviewer thought some of my comments too trenchant. I have tried to be careful, but in a survey this condensed I prefer to be a shade too trenchant than a good deal too bland. Apart from published reviews, I am indebted to several people who have written to me from various parts of the world to offer suggestions as to how to improve this *Survey*. To all of them I extend my gratitude.

Soli Deo gloria.

D. A. Carson
Trinity Evangelical Divinity School
March 2006

ABBREVIATIONS

Publishers named are those of the most recent editions in Britain and the USA. An entry such as (CUP) indicates that the book is published by CUP in both Britain and the USA. An entry with a "/"—e.g., (IVP/Eerdmans)—indicates it is published by IVP in Britain and by Eerdmans in the USA. (SCM/) means it is published in Britain by SCM and not published in the USA; (/Doubleday) that it is published by Doubleday in the USA and not published in Britain. The same symbol, the "/", is also used on occasion to divide British and American dates, British and American prices, and so forth—always in that paired order. Bookselling, like everything else, is being affected by the Internet: using plastic, a person anywhere can buy a book from anywhere and have it shipped anywhere. So if a book is sold, say, in the USA, and it is possible to record a "UK equivalent of the US list price," I have usually not bothered to do so: anyone can work out currency conversion. I have included both US and UK prices primarily when there are separate "list prices"—which may or may not converge.

Titles of commentaries are omitted when they are straightforward: e.g., Leon Morris, *The Gospel according to John: The English Text with Introduction, Exposition and Notes*, will appear as *Leon Morris* (i.e., with the author's name, rather than the book title, italicized). Where the title is a little unusual, the author's name will be in roman font and the title in italics, e.g., David deSilva, *Perseverance in Gratitude*.

AB	Anchor Bible (/Doubleday)
ACCS	Ancient Christian Commentary on Scripture: New Testament (/IVP)
ACNT	Augsburg Commentary on the New Testament
ANTC	Abingdon New Testament Commentary (/Abingdon)
ASV	American Standard Version
AV	Authorized Version
BBC	Blackwell Bible Commentary
BBR	*Bulletin of Biblical Research*
BCBC	Believers Church Bible Commentaries
BECNT	Baker Exegetical Commentary on the New Testament
BNTC	Black's New Testament Commentaries [=HNTC] (Black/Harper, sometimes Hendrickson)
BoT	Banner of Truth
BST	The Bible Speaks Today (IVP/IVP)
BTCB	Brazos Theological Commentary on the Bible
CB	Century Bible
CBC	Cambridge Bible Commentary on the NEB
CBSC	Cambridge Bible for Schools and Colleges
CC	The Communicator's Commentary (/Word)
CCT	Chalice Commentaries for Today
CGT	Cambridge Greek Testament (CUP)
ChB	The Church's Bible (Eerdmans)
CLC	Christian Literature Crusade
CNT	Commentaire du Nouveau Testament
CPNIVC	The College Press NIV Commentary
CUP	Cambridge University Press
DSB	Daily Study Bible (St Andrew/Westminster)
EB	The Expositor's Bible
EBC	The Expositor's Bible Commentary
ECC	Eerdmans Critical Commentary
EGGNT	Exegetical Guide to the Greek New Testament (/Eerdmans)
EGT	Expositor's Greek Testament
EKK	Evangelisch-katholisch Kommentar
ESV	English Standard Version
ET	English Translation
EtBib	Etudes Bibliques
FoB	Focus on the Bible (Christian Focus Publications/)
GNC	Good News Commentary (/Harper and Row)

hb	hardback
Hermeneia	Hermeneia: A Critical and Historical Commentary (SCM/ Fortress)
HNTC	Harper's New Testament Commentaries [=BNTC]
IB	Interpreter's Bible (SPCK/Abingdon)
IBT	Interpreting Biblical Texts (/Abingdon)
ICC	International Critical Commentary (T&T Clark/sometimes Scribner's)
IRT	Issues in Religion and Theology
IVPNTC	IVP New Testament Commentary (/IVP)
KJV	King James Version
KPG	Knox Preaching Guides (/John Knox)
LABC	Life Application Bible Commentary (/Tyndale House Publishers)
LBBC	Layman's Bible Book Commentaries (/Broadman)
MBC	Mellen Biblical Commentary
MBS	Message of Biblical Spirituality (Glazier/Liturgical)
MeyerK	Meyer Kommentar (Göttingen: Vandenhoeck und Ruprecht)
MMS	Marshall, Morgan and Scott
NAC	New American Commentary (Broadman & Holman)
NCB	New Century Bible
NCBC	New Cambridge Bible Commentary (CUP)
NClar	New Clarendon Commentary on the NEB (OUP)
nd	no date
NEB	New English Bible
NIB	The New Interpreter's Bible (Abingdon)
NIBC	New International Bible Commentary (Paternoster/ Hendrickson)
NIC (=NL)	New International Commentary (=New London) (some Hodder/all Eerdmans)
NIGTC	New International Greek Testament Commentary (Paternoster/Eerdmans)
NIV	New International Version
NIVAC	NIV Application Commentary
NIVNTC	NIV New Testament Commentary
NL	New London Commentary: see NIC
NovTSup	Supplements to *Novum Testamentum*
np	no price known
NRSV	New Revised Standard Version

13

NT	New Testament
NTC	New Testament Commentary (by Hendriksen and Kistemaker; BoT (for Hendriksen)/Baker; sometimes Evangelical Press (for Kistemaker)/Baker
NTG	New Testament Guides (Cornell/JSOT Press)
NTLNTM	New Testament Library (Westminster John Knox)
NTM	New Testament Message series (Veritas [Dublin]/Glazier [Liturgical]
NTSR	New Testament for Spiritual Reading
NTT	New Testament Theology (CUP)
op	out of print
OUP	Oxford University Press
pb	paperback
PBC	People's Bible Commentary (Concordia)
Pelican	Pelican Commentaries (Penguin, sometimes SCM/Penguin, sometimes Westminster)
Pillar	Pillar New Testament Commentaries (IVP/Eerdmans)
ProcC	Proclamation Commentaries (/Fortress)
RSV	Revised Standard Version
SAP	Sheffield Academic Press
SBLMS	Society of Biblical Literature Monograph Series
SIL	Summer Institute of Linguistics
SNTSMS	Society for New Testament Studies Monograph Series (CUP)
SP	Sacra Pagina (/Liturgical)
TBC	Torch Biblical Commentaries (SCM/Allenson)
TEV	Today's English Version
THNTC	Two Horizons New Testament Commentary
TNTC	Tyndale New Testament Commentaries (IVP/Eerdmans)
TPI	Trinity Press International
TPINT	Trinity Press International New Testament Commentaries (SCM/TPI)
UBS	United Bible Societies
UPA	University Press of America
WBC	Word Biblical Commentary (/Word)
WBComp	Westminster Bible Companion (Westminster John Knox)
WC	Westminster Commentaries
WUNT	Wissenschaftliche Untersuchungen zum Neuen Testament

1

INTRODUCTORY NOTES

1.1 The need for several types of commentary

For an effective teaching and preaching ministry, commentaries take their place among other essential tools. But since different tasks often require different tools, useful commentaries are of more than one kind. Those listed in this little book may serve in at least three or four distinct ways, which correspond to the following needs.

The dominant need is *to understand meanings accurately*. Postmodern sensibilities notwithstanding, the issue at stake is that of sheer faithfulness to the biblical message rather than smuggling one's own ideas into the interpretation under the cover of the authoritative text. Even so, commentaries in this category can be subdivided further. Some commentaries seek to establish the text and provide basic help in translation, choosing among variant readings and offering elementary help at the level of Greek syntax and semantics. Grammatical and linguistic commentaries help to ensure faithfulness to the meanings of words and phrases in their literary setting. Theological commentaries set words and phrases in the wider context of chapters, books, corpora, and even the canon. Of course, these three sub-categories often overlap—indeed, they *should* do so, for it can be seriously misleading to try to understand a word or concept in isolation from its linguistic and theological context.

To understand a passage (let alone to expound it forcefully) often requires *a faithful and imaginative historical reconstruction of events*. Actions and sayings cannot accurately be cashed into today's currency until the preacher (although not necessarily the congregation) has seen what these presuppose and involve in their original setting in the ancient world. The best response to those who argue that history, archaeology, and other related disciplines are irrelevant to the interpretative enterprise is to give them a copy of, say, Colin J. Hemer, *The Letters to the Seven Churches* (JSOT 1986/Eisenbrauns 1990) and suggest that they revise their theory. Rightly done, this kind of study contributes toward a vivid, colorful, and honest reconstruction for the congregation or classroom. Admittedly, it is disastrous when historical information becomes an end in itself (cf. the warning, "Divinity was easy; for 'divinity' meant Noah's Ark."). But even purely historical commentaries can do a useful job if they project readers faithfully into the ancient world.

Unfortunately, not a few commentaries in this camp attempt historical reconstructions that are long on speculation and short on even-handed weighing of evidence. Some of these historical reconstructions have become so powerful that they serve as a grid to authenticate the primary sources: for example, because a consensus has been reached among some scholars about the flow of early church history, the biblical documents are forcefully squeezed into the theory and counterevidence is dismissed as anachronistic or the like. Moreover, these kinds of reconstructions are probably the most difficult theories to evaluate for those not trained in the primary sources.

Nevertheless, these commentaries often include histories of the text (including form- and redaction-critical analyses), plus information of a geographical, historical, cultic, and socio-cultural nature, that cannot easily be found and weighed elsewhere without doing a lot of work in the primary sources.

Some commentaries offer useful guidance on the *legitimate range of practical application*. If one danger is to read one's own applications into the passage, books of the sort already mentioned may serve as the remedy. But equally, most students and pastors must be reminded of the many directions in which practical lessons can be found. Expository lecturing is not the same thing as expository preaching; the Word must not only inform but also wound and heal, sing and sting. Some of the older commentaries are exemplary in their concern to apply the Scriptures to later readers. But these hints and helps must be reviewed in the light of strictly exegetical considerations, for practical concerns can so control the text that no one hears the Word of God. Worse, the search for relevance frequently degenerates into the trite or the trivial.

A few commentaries perform all of these functions, but they are rare and usually dated.

Finally, I must say something about series of books that a casual glance might mistake for commentaries but that are really something else. A case in point is the IBT series, to which occasional reference is made in the following pages. The volumes in this series provide useful treatment of (for instance) *The Gospel of Matthew* or *The Gospels and Letters of John*, but they are not commentaries. These volumes try to help students grasp the issues and methods surrounding the interpretation of the biblical texts at issue. They are a mix of history of interpretation, survey of themes, exposition of sample texts, brief comments on structure, and so forth. Briefer yet, but perhaps a little more upmarket than IBT, is the New Testament Guides series. Only rarely have I mentioned NTG volumes.

1.2 Individual commentaries or series?

1.2.1 General principles

Series are almost always uneven, and the temptation to collect uniform sets of volumes should be seen for what it sometimes is. Often an author writes an individual volume because he or she has something to say that is worth saying. By contrast, series are often farmed out by publishers to well-known and therefore very busy scholars for whom the invitation is merely part of a day's work. This does not call into question the value of any particular series; it is certainly not meant to brand all commentaries that belong to a series with the label of mediocrity. But it does mean that volumes in series should ideally be judged only on individual merit. Thus comments on the major NT series now available (e.g., BNTC/HNTC, ICC, Hermeneia, NIGTC, etc.) will be found not only in the following paragraphs but also below under individual authors. Sets prepared by one scholar are a different matter and are discussed below (1.4).

1.2.2 Series worth noting but not pursuing

A few series are worth identifying, even if only the exceptional volume in the series achieves mention in these pages. *The Living Word Commentary* (ed. E. Ferguson; Austin: Sweet) testifies to the effort of the noninstrumental Churches of Christ to provide elementary commentaries for their laypersons. The series is in some ways theologically akin to the Tyndale Old Testament and New Testament Commentaries but generally a shade lighter. It has no relation to the *Living Bible* except the similarity in name; it must also be distinguished from the *Living Word* series (IVP/), which is not so much an attempt at formal commentary as a series of lay-oriented expository studies full of application and life. *The Armoury Commentary* compiles many years of the Salvation Army's annual Bible Reading Notes. *Everyman's Bible Commentary* (/Moody) is too elementary to be very useful; *The Layman's Bible Commentary* (/John Knox) is singularly undistinguished. Collins/Fontana have come out with a series of thirteen books designed to explain "everything that really matters for the modern reader" of the NT. In some cases (e.g., Mark, Luke, John, Romans, Galatians), these are succinct commentaries on the TEV; elsewhere they provide essays (Acts) or brief introductions. They are elementary and sometimes misleading even if, on the whole, they are engagingly written. Pitched at about the same level, but for Southern Baptist readers, is the *Holman New Testament Commentary* series, only a few of whose growing list of entries are mentioned in these pages. Included are such matters as "life application," a prayer relating to the text, and sometimes a teaching outline and discussion questions. Fortress continues to publish its series *Proclamation Commentaries: The New Testament Witnesses for Preaching*. These short books, written by established scholars, are supposed to help the preacher come to grips with the essential themes of the NT documents. Occasional volumes from the series are mentioned in these notes, but as a rule the commentaries are not very helpful to the preacher interested in systematically expounding the Scriptures, even if they are useful handbooks for helping students discover the way much contemporary scholarship understands the biblical texts. In short, they are useful compendia for students; preachers interested in biblical exposition should begin with something more challenging. The *Knox Preaching Guides* series is no better; neither is *Interpretation Bible Studies* (/Geneva Press). The *Layman's Bible Book Commentary* (24 vols.; /Broadman) is very elementary and frequently resorts to slippery language to sound more conservative than it really is. The *Communicator's Commentary Series* (/Word) is a trifle better than those just mentioned, partly because the individual volumes are usually longer than those in the other series; but application is read back into the text with alarming frequency and with too little awareness of the hermeneutical steps being taken. At best these commentaries are worth a quick skim *after* the preacher's serious exegetical work is well in hand, in order to retrieve any homiletical stimulus that may be present. Another series too thin to merit much notice in these pages is the *College Press Bible Commentary Series*, a product of the Independent Christian Churches and the noninstrumental Churches of Christ. The volumes that have appeared so far are gently conservative, fairly consistently partisan to their theological heritage, and usually aimed at the lay student or poorly trained pastor, but they are not robust enough to be the primary support for well-trained students and preachers. There are a few exceptional volumes in the series, noted below. A new set, *The Complete Biblical Library*, edited by Ralph W. Harris (Springfield, MO: Gospel Publishing, 1991), is an extraordinary mélange. It includes an expanded interlinear (the *textus receptus* plus "important variants"), its own text-critical apparatus, various versions, and verse-by-verse commentary designed for the beginning layperson. In other words, the more technical material is almost useless to the lay reader, and the comments are so lacking in depth as to be almost useless to any mature reader, lay or otherwise. Some sections are better than others, but the series as a whole is too expensive ($639.20) for the little it offers. The *Free Will Baptist Commentary* (/Randall House) includes one or two volumes worth a quick skim (e.g., Jack W. Stallings on John) but is so elementary and so defensive on "free will" that it can safely be overlooked. The new *Focus on the Bible* commentary series (Christian Focus Publications/) is far from complete, but its volumes usually lie somewhere between the BST and the Tyndale Commentaries. The *Westminster Bible Companion* series (/Westminster John Knox) is an attempt to break into the popular-level market largely held by evangelicals (e.g., TNTC, IVPNTC). So far it does not approach the well-established series in either quality or reliability. The *Life Application Bible Commentary* (/Tyndale House Publishers) is a slimmer and more popular counterpart to the *NIVAC* (see below) with most of its weaknesses and few of its strengths. The series of *Feminist Companion* volumes to various biblical books continues to grow, written by Athalya Brenner on Old Testament books, and by Amy-Jill Levine and others on New Testament books. It will ordinarily not be noticed in the following pages, since the volumes offer comments only on those passages of relevance to that interest, not on the entire text. In other words, these volumes are "companions" to biblical texts, not commentaries on them. Moreover, despite the valid insights that frequently turn up in these companions, the approach, monofocal as it is, seems almost calculated to encourage misinterpretation of the text being studied.

Finally, a new series of books with titles all beginning with *The Teaching of* has been launched by Christian Focus/. Sponsored by the Proclamation Trust, this series is something of a new genre: part commentary, part sample expositions of select passages, part summary of themes—all in brief compass and all designed to help the preacher think through how to preach from the biblical book in question. I have included only one volume of the series in these notes (Lucas and Philip on John).

1.2.3 More substantial series

Better known and more substantial series, whose individual volumes normally receive separate treatment in the pages of this book, include the following:

The *Abingdon New Testament Commentaries* (/Abingdon) are designed to be "compact, critical commentaries on the writings of the New Testament." They are written with the theological student in mind but are reasonably accessible to others. By including sections on literary genre and structure, they have a more contemporary feel than some older commentaries. By and large, however, their interaction with alternative interpretations is thin—and this can be more than a little irritating when of various possible interpretations, the reader's interpretation of the passage is not even mentioned, and more than a little dangerous when the reader is not made aware that there are alternatives.

The *Ancient Christian Commentary on Scripture: New Testament* (/IVP), edited by Thomas C. Oden, brings together in fresh translation passages from the patristics that comment on biblical books. The unwary—those largely ignorant of the patristic contexts—may be lured into misappropriation of ostensible parallels. The better trained will find this series a wonderful resource for expanding their horizons.

The *Anchor Bible* (/Doubleday) is a decidedly mixed series. It is ecumenical, moderately critical, and designed to extend through both Testaments, including the Apocrypha. Each volume offers introduction, a new translation, linguistic and exegetical notes, and sometimes a more detailed exposition. But the length and complexity of the treatment vary enormously: e.g., Brown on John and on the Johannine Epistles is immensely detailed, while Albright and Mann on Matthew have produced a volume with a lengthy introduction and almost no exegesis.

The *Baker Exegetical Commentary on the New Testament* is a large-scale project, in some ways rivaling the NIGNT series: both in the degree of interaction with secondary literature and in its reliance on the Greek text, BECNT is a major evangelical contribution. At the same time, because it provides the Greek both in Greek font and in transliteration, translates any foreign-language expression, and is edited for readability, the series aims to draw readers all the way from serious scholars to pastors and students to "the motivated lay Christian who craves a solid but accessible exposition." Protestations of readability aside, I suspect that most readers will be serious pastors, students, and scholars. More than some series, BECNT tries to integrate exegesis and serious confessional theological reflection.

The *Believers Church Bible Commentary* is the product of Mennonites (in particular, Mennonite Brethren) with a high view of Scripture, a commitment to the "believers church" tradition, and (usually) a gently Arminian soteriology. The series is accessible, pious in the best sense, but rarely at the front rank.

The series of *Black New Testament Commentaries/Harper New Testament Commentaries* aims to provide lucid comment on the NT text and a fresh translation without requiring a detailed knowledge of Greek. A few of the volumes in the series are distinguished (e.g., Barrett on 1 and 2 Corinthians). On the American side some of the volumes in the series have been taken over by Hendrickson. New volumes to replace earlier entries are being published on the American side only by Hendrickson, so the "H" in HNTC has changed its referent!

The *Blackwell Bible Commentaries* series is very new. It aims to cover every book in the Bible. Only a few NT volumes have appeared so far: see Edwards on John and Rowland on Revelation. The series is innovative: it is devoted primarily to the "reception history" of each book of the Bible, "based on the premiss that how people have interpreted, and been influenced by, a sacred text like the Bible is often as interesting and historically important as what it originally meant." The aim is to reflect on the influence of the Bible on literature, but also on art, music, and film. The series will prove both interesting and useful if it expands the horizons of readers who might otherwise be rather narrowly locked into the present, but not for a moment should we sanction the view that each "reception" of the text is as valid as any other "reception."

The *Brazos Theological Commentary on the Bible* has just been launched (see Jaroslav Pelikan on Acts, below). It aims to provide rich theology in reasonably compact space, ignoring most of the debates kicked up by historical criticism and increasingly viewed as arid. The concern is not unjustified, but the reaction may be a bit over the top: the fact is that so much of God's gracious self-disclosure in the Scripture lies in actions and words that are powerfully embedded *in history*, so that the historical dimension must not be marginalized too hastily. Certainly the series bears watching.

The *Broadman Bible Commentary* is a product of scholars related to the Southern Baptist Convention (SBC). The series is compact, expository, not technical, not particularly insightful, frequently bland, and sometimes speculative. The reformation in the ranks of the SBC during the last two decades has dictated that an alternative and more conservative series, *The New American Commentary*, be produced by the same press. Quite a few volumes have now appeared. Its authors have been drawn from Baptist ranks both within and outside the SBC. The early volumes are generally competent enough, pitched at a middle level.

The Church's Bible, edited by Robert Louis Wilken, is a new undertaking that probes how the biblical books were interpreted in the first centuries. Transparently it is akin to the ACCS series (see above) but is somewhat more technical. Only one volume has appeared so far (see Kovacs on 1 Corinthians).

The *College Press NIV Commentary* has a slightly misleading name, since College Press is a product of the Restorationist movement. This series is an attempt to break into a slightly more scholarly market. Most of the contributions that have appeared so far are decidedly on the light side, but some of the volumes are stronger.

The *Eerdmans Critical Commentary* is fairly recent, with only two volumes out so far, both published in 2000. It promises to be a major undertaking, rivaling ICC or the larger volumes of AB for its attention to detail, and adopting a moderately liberal stance. For the two initial volumes, see comments on Philemon and on the Pastorals.

The *Epworth Preachers Commentaries* is a series more exegetical than expository, but too brief to be of great help. The series is taking on new life: after several years with no new volumes, a spate of them has appeared during the past decade and a half. It is more interested in narrative structures than in helping preachers, but it is certainly worth scanning.

The Expositor's Bible Commentary (/Zondervan) is a twelve-volume work of large pages and small print designed to offer exegetical and expository comment on the entire Bible, using the NIV text as the basis. The NT portion embraces vols. 8–12. The series is committed to evangelicalism but suffers serious unevenness—a flaw made worse by the fact that more than one NT book commentary is bound in each volume (e.g., the synoptics in vol. 8, John and Acts in vol. 9, etc.). It is usually more technical than the old EB (1887–96). In recent printings, individual commentaries have appeared in paperback or bound with others in paperback. The publisher is committed to bringing out a substantially revised edition of the series, and the first of the revised volumes, vol. 13 covering Hebrews–Revelation, has just appeared (so the series will become a thirteen-volume set instead of a twelve-volume set). All the contributors are new, and the typeface is much more pleasing.

Though seriously dated, the five volumes of the old *Expositor's Greek Testament* are still worth owning and reading along with more recent works. Pick it up secondhand, as it is now once again out of print.

Hermeneia (SCM/Fortress) is a full-scale critical commentary series that devotes considerable attention to parallel texts. Unlike the ICC, allowance is made for readers without a classical education by providing translations (usually from the Loeb edition) of cited Greek and Latin authors. Several of the volumes are translations of German works, and initially this included some extremely dated books (e.g., Bultmann on the Johannine Epistles), but these are being replaced (in this instance by a major commentary written by Strecker). Haenchen on John, however, should have been put out to pasture long ago. "Parallelomania" (to use Sandmel's famous expression) and a naive appeal to history-of-religions assumptions frequently surface in the volumes of this series, but the series remains invaluable for the serious exegete and expositor. A few volumes are outstanding (e.g., Attridge on Hebrews).

The *International Critical Commentary*, a project more than a century old, is now being renewed. The old volumes include some major commentaries that still set a high standard, even if they are now seriously dated. Greek and Latin texts are cited without translation: this will prove a drawback to many modern readers. Only a few volumes of the modern updating have appeared, but they are of exceptional quality (see notes on Cranfield on Romans, Davies and Allison on Matthew, Barrett on Acts)—though so pricey as to be beyond the reach of many students and pastors.

The *Interpretation* series of commentaries (/John Knox) focuses less on detailed exegesis than on the thrust and themes of the biblical books, presented in a way best calculated to help the preacher and to relate the text to a wider context. The aim is admirable; the execution is mixed, partly because the thinness of the exegesis sometimes allows room for rather too much speculation.

The *Interpreter's Bible* (SPCK/Abingdon) is a well-intended but largely failed project to mingle historical scholarship and homiletical hints. Its successor, the *New Interpreter's Bible* (/Abingdon), is considerably stronger. Its contributors vary more substantially than do the contributors to most series—both in their theological stance and in the level at which they write.

The *IVP New Testament Commentaries* (/IVP) are designed to fit into the fairly narrow slot between the TNTC and the BST—in other words, they are still commentaries, but they are brief, simple, and designed to be immediately nurturing. Quite a few have now appeared, and if several are bland, several others are outstanding (W. Larkin on Acts, I. Howard Marshall on 1 Peter, Linda Belleville on 2 Corinthians, Rodney Whitacre on John).

The *Moffatt* series, with rare exceptions, is not much more than a major disappointment.

The *New Cambridge Bible Commentary* (CUP), based on the NRSV, "aims to elucidate the Hebrew and Christian Scriptures for a wide range of intellectually curious individuals." [Picky observation: in the name of political correctness, the disjunctive quality of an expression like "Hebrew and Christian Scriptures" suggests that "Christian Scriptures" refers only to documents of the New Testament. Marcion triumphs.] Only a few volumes have appeared so far, and they are tilted toward the extensive use of rhetorical criticism, narrative criticism, and social-scientific tools. Granted such focus, the volumes are happily accessible but not in the front rank.

The *New Century Bible* (MMS/Eerdmans) normally adopts a moderately critical stance. Primary attention is devoted to understanding what the text says without raising many broader theological, expository, or other concerns. Some of the volumes in the series are dry; a few offer excellent value for the money.

The *New International Biblical Commentary* (/Hendrickson) has adapted the old GNC series to the NIV and is still adding new volumes. On the whole it is competent without being technical or overly long. Only some of the volumes in this series will receive comment in the pages that follow.

New Testament Guides (Cornell/JSOT) are so slim that they rarely receive notice in the pages that follow.

The *New Testament Message* (/Michael Glazier) is a Catholic series of slim books that vary between being, more or less, commentaries (working through the text roughly paragraph by paragraph) and thematic surveys.

A new series of *Narrative Commentaries* (Epworth/TPI) may become, in the NT, the American equivalent of the revised *Epworth Preachers Commentaries*. On the whole, it is disappointing.

The *New Clarendon Bible* on the NEB has ground to a halt. Only a few volumes were published, and no more are projected. That is probably a good thing: the books that appeared were too brief and too bland to be useful—again with one or two notable exceptions.

The *New International Commentary on the New Testament* (/Eerdmans; sometimes referred to in the UK as the *New London Commentary*, MMS/) is a still-incomplete series of commentaries that adopts conservative critical views and is concerned to offer an exegesis of the Scriptures themselves. The text of these commentaries demands no special knowledge; the footnotes presuppose some knowledge of Greek and (occasionally) Hebrew and Latin. With the death of F. F. Bruce, its editor for many years, editorial direction passed to Gordon D. Fee, who has commissioned writers not only to complete the series but to prepare new volumes to replace some of the older entries (e.g., Moo on Romans, replacing Murray).

The *New International Greek Testament Commentary* (Paternoster/ Eerdmans) is up-to-date, bibliographically almost exhaustive, exegetical, and within the evangelical tradition, broadly understood. Volumes keep appearing, some of them outstanding. One or two volumes have been criticized, not unfairly, by clergy who find their contents too technical and tightly packed to be useful. For clergy and others well trained in Greek and exegesis, the series is one to watch.

The *NIV Application Commentary* series (/Zondervan) provides fairly lightweight commentaries, easily accessible, that are then filled out by application of various kinds. At one level this aim is commendable: it works against the view that biblical interpretation has the right to remain a cool and distanced discipline with the interpreter standing over the text. Yet there are converse dangers. Shallow handling of the Word coupled with immediate application may unwittingly foster the view that Scripture has primarily utilitarian value. The applications themselves may be driven by many different agendas, so that false connections are constructed between text and application. Lazy preachers may so rely on the applications provided by this series that they fail to devote themselves to the hard work of cultural reflection and appropriate application—just as lazy preachers may so rely on the immediate conclusions of commentaries in general that they never really learn how to do exegesis. Once its limitations and dangers are acknowledged, however, this series can be a useful pump-primer in the move from text to application.

The *Pelican* series is generally undistinguished, but it boasts a few commentaries that are quite outstanding, including Sweet's work on the Apocalypse (now available in the USA as the *TPI New Testament Commentary* series).

The *Pillar Commentary Series* (/Eerdmans) started life as a non-series. Eerdmans published three independent commentaries (Carson on John, Morris on Romans, Hughes on Revelation) and put them all in the same binding. They then decided it was worth filling out an entire series, and the other NT books have now been commissioned. Several further volumes have appeared, with more on the way.

Preaching the Word is the title of a series of expository works, edited by R. Kent Hughes, designed to cover every book of the Bible. Because these expositions go right through the biblical book being covered, each volume can be pretty substantial. Strictly speaking, these books are not commentaries, but because they belong to the vision of exposition that systematically works through texts, they do comment on the thrust of each passage, and sometimes on the details, while providing models of how to expound Scripture within this homiletical tradition. The English Bible used is either the NIV or the ESV. They should not be any preacher's first recourse, but it is highly salutary for preachers to learn how fellow preachers have handled the same text—provided, of course, that such material does not become an excuse for plagiarism.

For comparative purposes, it is sometimes worth using the indexes at sermoncentral.com.

Sacra Pagina is a relatively new series edited by Daniel J. Harrington, SJ. (/Liturgical). The volumes released so far reflect the best of modern critical Catholic scholarship. The commentaries include fresh translation, critical analysis, and theologically sensitive exposition within the Roman Catholic tradition. They vary more than many series in the depth of coverage they provide: more so than for many series, buy only the best volumes.

Standard Bible Studies (/Standard Publishing) is a series of commentaries designed for the ordinary reader. Most of these books reflect a very poor level of competence. The volume by Paul R. McReynolds on Mark is an attractive exception.

The *Two Horizons New Testament Commentary* is a new series (see Fowl on Philippians) that is seeking to bridge the gap between biblical studies and systematic theology. It aims to read the New Testament texts theologically, section by section (rather than verse by verse or phrase by phrase).

The *Torch Bible Commentaries* are brief, exegetical, and sometimes theological; but frequently the help they provide is too lean precisely where it is most needed.

The *Tyndale New Testament Commentaries* are designed for the frequently-targeted well-read layperson, but many pastors profit as well. The series is conservative but focuses most attention on explaining the meaning of the text with minimal interaction with the voluminous secondary literature. Originally based on the AV/KJV, with Greek and Hebrew transliterated and explained, the series is being rewritten based on the RSV or NIV (at the individual author's discretion), and space is being assigned more equitably. Several of the volumes of this new edition are, within the constraints of the series, outstanding (e.g., Marshall on Acts).

The *Wesleyan Bible Commentary* is a six-volume work published in 1979 and reprinted in 1986 (/Hendrickson). It is "a set of commentaries within the Wesleyan frame of reference," and uses the ASV. The series is not technical, and most sections are written with warmth and piety.

Unfortunately, the competence of the authors is quite variable, and most of the work was seriously dated before it went to press.

The *Westminster Commentaries* are dull, dated, and dry.

The *Word Biblical Commentary* is a full-scale series that aims to cover every book in the Bible. The series offers fresh translation, an original (and annoyingly repetitive) format, thoughtful interaction with the literature, and a commitment to handle both exegetical and literary/critical concerns. A few of the volumes that have appeared are already standard reference works. Do not let the "evangelical" label fool you: although some of the contributors sit comfortably within that tradition, in other cases the label applies only by the most generous extension.

The *Zondervan Illustrated Bible Backgrounds Commentary* is a four-volume work edited by Clinton E. Arnold (2002, £23.99 per vol., £95.99 for the set/$39.99 per vol., $159.99 for the set). It is sometimes worth skimming in conjunction with commentaries on the text at hand, but the best of the major commentaries usually include all the relevant background materials anyway. To use this four-volume set by itself is unwise: it might encourage the unwary reader to think that the background is the foreground, with the result that what the text actually says quietly dissolves from view.

1.2.4 One-volume multi-author commentaries

One-volume commentaries are too brief to be useful in detailed exegesis and exposition, but they have the advantage of providing at least *something* on every book of the Bible—an advantage when the student or minister is young or able to maintain only a very small library. The *New Bible Commentary* (IVP/Eerdmans, latest revision 1994) is condensed, evangelical, and brief. It is primarily exegetical, but a little space is devoted to discussing critical theories and occasionally to ongoing application of the text. In its various editions it has become something of a standard around the English-speaking world among evangelical readers of single-volume commentaries. Several other volumes have aimed for more or less the same evangelical market. Some of them deserve honorable mention: *A Bible Commentary for Today* (Pickering and Inglis/ 1979) = *The New Layman's Bible Commentary* (/Zondervan

1979) is a product of the Christian Brethren. Based on the RSV, its focus is sometimes on exegesis, sometimes on exposition. On the whole it is lighter than the *New Bible Commentary*. One should not overlook the latest revision of *International Bible Commentary* (/Zondervan 1986), edited by F. F. Bruce. The *Evangelical Commentary on the Bible*, edited by Walter A. Elwell, is useful (/Baker 1989). *The Zondervan NIV Bible Commentary* is in two volumes, but its second volume is devoted to the NT (/Zondervan 1994). With one fat volume devoted to the last quarter of the canon, inevitably it offers a little more comment per line of text than the one-volume commentaries on the whole Bible.

Until a quarter of a century ago, the standard one-volume mainstream critical commentary was probably *Peake's Commentary* (Nelson, revised 1962; now published by Routledge 2002, £35.00/$59.95). It should not be confused with the 1919 edition, which is still sold secondhand. Nowadays, however, it has been eclipsed by *Harper's Bible Commentary* (Harper and Row 1990/1988); *The Interpreter's One-Volume Commentary on the Bible* (/Abingdon), not to be confused with IB; *Mercer Commentary on the Bible* (/Mercer 1995); and especially *The New Jerome Biblical Commentary* (G. Chapman/Prentice Hall 1989/1990). The latter two also treat the Apocrypha. The fairly recent "Catholic and ecumenical" one-volume commentary, edited by William Farmer and David L. Dungan, is *The International Bible Commentary* (/Liturgical Press 1998). On critical issues it is all over the map. It begins with several essays on contemporary subjects (e.g., "The Bible in the Charismatic Movement," "Family: An African Perspective," and "The Bible and Ecology"), but perhaps its most intriguing characteristic is that its international cast of authors write from their own national perspectives, such that those from the Two-Thirds World may not make even passing reference to Western critical concerns. The *Eerdmans Commentary on the Bible*, edited by James D. G. Dunn and John Rogerson (Eerdmans 2003, £42.99/$75.00) will find its niche and possibly displace some of the ones just mentioned.

In a class by itself is the *Women's Bible Commentary*, ed. by Carol A. Newson and Sharon H. Ringe (/Westminster John Knox 1992). It is not a commentary on the whole Bible but on those passages and themes that either mention women or are judged by the authors to be of special relevance to women. Thus the section on John treats 2:1–11; 4:4–42; 7:53–8:11; 11:1–44; 12:1–9; 19:25–27; 20:1–18 (so far as Mary Magdalene is the focus of interest), and offers comments on, e.g., the use of "Father" for addressing God. Despite some excellent insights here and there, the work as a whole is far less interested in hearing what Scripture says than in using it to bless the controlling axioms of the more radical edge of the feminist movement.

Equally hard to classify, if for different reasons, is the *Hellenistic Commentary to the New Testament* (/Abingdon 1995, $70.00), edited by M. Eugene Boring, Klaus Berger, and Carsten Colpe. It is not a commentary in any traditional sense. Rather, it works in canonical order through a large selection of NT texts and provides ostensible parallels from the Hellenistic sources. The undiscerning will use it and fall into what Samuel Sandmel used to call "parallelomania"; nevertheless, busy students and preachers who do not have ready access to obscure sources may find it a help. Less helpful is the one-volume NT commentary by M. Eugene Boring and Fred B. Craddock, *The People's New Testament: Commentary* (/Westminster John Knox, $19.95). Its mix of backgrounds, exegesis, and homiletical tips might have made this work outstanding. Instead, far too often the interpretation is controlled by debatable reconstructions, and the homiletical helps reflect a rather domesticated theology.

1.3 Older commentaries

The present notes tend to concentrate on recent books, especially since useful guides are available to the older classics (e.g., the guide by Spurgeon). On the Greek text, some of the older commentators, including Westcott and Lightfoot, tended to overlook the distinctive fluidity of Hellenistic Greek as over against the more precisely defined constructions of the classical era; that aside, to those whose Greek is reasonably good Westcott and Lightfoot always repay careful study. *Geoffrey Wilson* has compiled "digests of Reformed comment" on most of the NT books. Published in paperback by BoT (whose prices, especially in the UK, remain gratifyingly low), these slim volumes provide useful distillations of Calvin and other magisterial reformers, and of some of the Puritans, with occasional snippets from more recent writers (including Lightfoot and Stott). The comments are often apposite and spiritually stimulating, but of course these books must be used in conjunction with major exegetical works. Very recently BoT has combined these slim digests together into two volumes of *New Testament Commentaries*, vol. 1 covering Romans to Ephesians, and vol. 2 covering Philippians to Hebrews plus Revelation (2005). Zondervan recently reprinted *J. P. Lange*'s commentaries in twelve volumes, but it is again op.

Klock and Klock Publishing Co., which used to serve us well with limited edition reprints of important commentaries, is now listed in *Books in Print* as "Inactive/Out of Business." Apparently some stock has been taken over by Kregel. Many of these older commentaries that were available for a few years are now regrettably op, including *P. Fairbairn* on the Pastorals, *F. J. A. Hort* on 1 Peter, and *James B. Mayor* on James. BoT keeps *Matthew Poole* in print. The third volume, which covers the books of the New Testament, was reprinted most recently in 1996.

Some patristic commentaries are bound up with volumes of *The Ante-Nicene, Nicene, and Post-Nicene Fathers*. *Calvin*'s commentaries are available in various reprint editions of older translations. Perhaps the least expensive access is in the Baker set (/$200.00); consider also the twelve-volume edition put out by Eerdmans ($21.95 per vol., $260.00 for the set). Some of Calvin's commentaries are available from BoT. New translations are in preparation. *Matthew Henry*'s work, originally written to complement the work of Matthew Poole, is available on the British side in a one-volume edition from Marshall Pickering (£29.99), and in a two-volume paperback from Hodder (£3.95 each). On the American side, both Zondervan and Hendrickson have produced one-volume editions (out of stock and $29.97 respectively). Marshall Pickering/Zondervan have brought out a modernized edition of Matthew Henry that many readers will doubtless appreciate. Revised and edited by Gerald Peterman, it sells under the title *Matthew Henry's Commentary on the NIV: Genesis—Revelation* (1993). Both Calvin and Henry are still worth reading. The latter makes shrewd, practical comments; the former is a more reliable interpreter of Scripture. Both should be used only in conjunction with modern commentators.

1.4 One-author sets

A. T. Robertson's *Word Pictures of the New Testament* (originally 6 vols., now 9 vols.; /Baptist Sunday School Board [1982], $110.00) provides comments on the more important Greek words of the NT text in a way that often brings them to life, but sometimes he is dangerously near irresponsible etymologizing (cf. the warnings of James Barr in his *The Semantics of Biblical Language*). Only rarely, however, is there a howler. The magnificent achievement of *H. A. W. Meyer* in the last century has been reprinted in ET: 11 fat volumes with a total of 7,050 pp. (/Hendrickson), but it is again out of print. Of course these commentaries should not be used independently of more recent ones.

J. C. Ryle's *Expository Thoughts on the Gospels* are still being reprinted—in seven volumes by BoT (/$79.95 or $12.95 per vol.), in four volumes (Evangelical Press/Crossway, though op in the UK, assorted prices from $15.99 to $17.99 per volume in the US), and in three volumes (J. Clarke/ [Matthew and Mark in the same volume]; each volume is either £15.00 or £17.00). The series is devout, militantly Protestant, and down-to-earth. His thoughts are simple (often too simple) but telling. At least they are thoroughly practical and directly serve the preacher.

Albert Barnes, *Notes on the New Testament* (/Kregel in one vol., $54.79; /Baker in 14 vols., $670.00) marries common sense and pungent practicality but every so often resorts to eccentric exegesis. *C. Erdman*'s seventeen volumes on the NT (op) are lightweight but sometimes worth a quick skim. R. C. H. Lenski's twelve-volume *The Interpretation of the New Testament* (/Augsburg Fortress, $29.99 per vol.—but most of the volumes are op) aims to force the student to think through the Greek text and stimulate exegetical rigor, but his grasp of Greek is mechanical, amateurish, and without respect for the fluidity of Greek in the Hellenistic period. The series is marred by a militant or even angry tone in defense of orthodox Lutheranism.

William Barclay's *Daily Study Bible* covers the entire NT in eighteen volumes. The second revised edition (1993) is available on both sides of the Atlantic (St. Andrews/Westminster John Knox, £100.00 pb for the set or £8.99 per vol./$199.95 pb for the set or $29.95 per vol.). The series is also available in a "less deluxe" edition (/Crossway, $99.95). Its value for the expositor is enormous; Barclay is eminently quotable and could not be dull if he tried. But two tendencies should be noted by way of warning: Barclay often maximizes "spiritual" application from the text after minimizing the historical foundation (e.g., miracles tend to be lessons *rather than* events); and sometimes one wonders whether the text bears all the applications suggested. But the minister who can find foundations elsewhere will enjoy Barclay's superstructure, even if some of the more dashing frescoes should be ignored.

A series not worth purchasing is the eighteen-volume *Renaissance New Testament* by Randolph O. Yeager (/Pelican, $25.00 per vol.). Each hardback volume is close to 600 pages long, and the series occupied Yeager for fifty years; but the result is a disappointing monument to misplaced energy. The work is based on the KJV; many Greek words have concordance references provided for them, duplicating tools that already exist; most terms are parsed. The comments are shallow, the prose turgid, and comment on Greek syntax too frequently misguided.

Considerably better is the series of commentaries by *William Hendriksen* (NTC). Eight volumes were produced: Matthew, Mark, Luke, John, Romans, Galatians-Ephesians, Philippians-Colossians-Philemon, and Thessalonians-Timothy-Titus (BoT, mostly out of print/Baker, ranging from $39.99 to $49.99 per volume). Hendriksen is self-consciously orthodox and Reformed. Although his comments are often helpful to the expositor, the verbosity of his style and the selectivity of his interaction with alternative interpretations demand that he be supplemented with other works. Nevertheless, his concern for practical application can make his work useful to some preachers. In the wake of Hendriksen's death, *Simon Kistemaker* agreed to complete the series, and all the volumes have now appeared (/Baker, ranging from $39.99 to $49.99 per volume; $250.00 for the complete set of Hendriksen and Kistemaker). On the British side, only two volumes have been picked up, both by Evangelical Press: the one on Hebrews (£17.95), and the one on James, 1–2 Peter, 1–3 John, and Jude (£19.99). On the whole, his work is solid but not incisive, with the result that there are usually better alternatives.

Several one-volume, single-author commentaries sport peculiar strengths and weaknesses. Craig S. Keener, *The IVP Bible Background*

Commentary: New Testament (/IVP 1994, $32.00) does not so much comment on the entire text as offer comment on those parts of the text he judges to be best elucidated by referring to "background" material—or, more precisely, such texts become the springboard for elucidating that background material (which may be textual, archaeological, social, and so forth). Alister McGrath, *The NIV Bible Companion: A Basic Commentary* (/Zondervan 1997) is so brief (basic?) that it is not very helpful for any but the merest beginner. The *NIV Compact Bible Commentary* (/Zondervan 1999, $19.99), by John Sailhamer, is about 50 percent longer but nevertheless very short. Its idiosyncratic readings of canonical connections are sometimes very stimulating, sometimes overblown and unwarranted. *The Victor Bible Background Commentary: New Testament*, by Lawrence O. Richards (/Communications Ministries 1994, $32.99), is too unreliable to earn a recommendation. The *Bible Knowledge Commentary: Old Testament and New Testament* by John Walvoord (/Chariot Victor 1989, $89.99) comments out of the framework of classic dispensationalism.

2

Supplements to Commentaries

In the first two editions of this little book, a few notes were included in this section offering bibliographical suggestions on parables, NT theologies, Bible and theological dictionaries, and one or two other matters. In the third edition I eliminated such notes since the work focuses primarily on commentaries, and to include many other matters would demand that this section be greatly expanded. I have retained only two subsections: one dealing with NT introductions and another with NT theologies, and in both cases I provide merely representative coverage, not an exhaustive survey.

2.1 New Testament introductions

Many New Testament introductions have appeared in the last few years. From the conservative stable, the most detailed volume is still the earlier mammoth work by Donald Guthrie, *New Testament Introduction*, in its fourth edition (IVP 1990, £32.99/IVP, $45.00). There were few critical questions in his own day that Guthrie did not discuss, but inevitably his work is becoming a little dated. Guthrie's style is invariably irenic, his conclusions normally traditional. Relatively little space is given to the theological contribution of each NT book, or to struggling with the actual history of early Christianity. Nothing in the work orients the reader to the social sciences, for instance, and there is little wrestling with ancient schools of rhetoric. The entire volume is given over to traditional topics of "introduction." Moreover, occasionally the sheer volume of detail may make it difficult for students to sort out what is most important. Nevertheless, Guthrie's *Introduction* is still an important reference work. An excellent complement to Guthrie is the work by Lee Martin McDonald and Stanley E. Porter, *Early Christianity and Its Sacred Literature* (/Hendrickson 2000, $39.95). This is a major work that attempts to ground the documents of the New Testament in the history and culture of the Jewish and Greco-Roman world of the first two centuries.

A slightly more compact work, and one that is better designed to serve as a textbook for theological students, is the very recent book *An Introduction to the New Testament* by D. A. Carson and Douglas J. Moo (/Zondervan 2005, $39.99). This replaces the earlier edition by Carson, Moo, and Morris. Although it focuses primarily on matters of introduction (and provides references for many of the patristic sources that contemporary NT introductions tend to ignore), it also attempts to summarize the theological contribution of each book of the NT and interact with some contemporary issues (e.g., the new perspective on Paul) and perennial topics (e.g., the nature of pseudonymity). For undergraduates and lay beginners, perhaps the most attractive work is that of Walter A. Elwell and Robert W. Yarbrough, *Encountering the New Testament: A Historical and Theological Survey*, now in its second edition (/Baker 2005, $44.99)—a colorful book supplemented by an interactive CD. Now that it is out in paperback, the volume of learned essays by E. Earle Ellis, *The Making of the New Testament Documents* (Brill 2002, €49.00/$46.00), might be considered by more advanced readers. It is not a comprehensive introduction—this is really a collection of Ellis's essays—but the topics it chooses to handle are handled masterfully. The lengthy work by David A. deSilva, *An Introduction to the New Testament:*

Contexts, Methods & Ministry Formation (IVP 2004, £24.99/IVP 2004, $40.00) is harder to evaluate. It covers the standard "introduction" topics, but includes numerous "exegetical skills" sections covering a wide range of passages that deSilva interprets for the readers, and many additional sections in which he tries to tease out the relevance for ministry formation of various passages and books of the New Testament. I suspect that the book reflects the ways that deSilva himself teaches the New Testament. Others who teach it in this fashion will doubtless find the book helpful. But in colleges and seminaries where the curriculum is structured a bit differently, teachers may find deSilva's work frustrating. Very often I found myself disagreeing with his exegesis or with the cogency of the applications he was attempting. I started to wish there were space for more adequate discussion instead of the large quantity of conclusions with few or only shallow justifications. In other words, the strength of this book is its weakness: in order to achieve integration, it attempts many things but covers so many of them so lightly that informed readers will be unimpressed, while beginning students will not be exposed to the depth of the debate they need.

Probably the premier mainstream critical work is that of Raymond E. Brown, *An Introduction to the New Testament* (/Doubleday 1997, $49.50). In sweep of coverage within that tradition, it is unsurpassed. It has now largely displaced Werner Georg Kümmel, *Introduction to the New Testament* (SCM, £22.50/Abingdon, $35.00). In Kümmel, the comprehensiveness of the topics discussed, in relatively little space, means that far too many opinions are advanced without defense. One should not overlook Luke Timothy Johnson, *The Writings of the New Testament*, especially its third edition (SCM 2003, £39.99/Augsburg Fortress 2002, $39.00). It is moderate in tone and full of the clarity and sense many have come to expect from its author. Occupying approximately the same conceptual space, but neither as penetrating nor as engaging, is the work jointly written by Paul Achtemeier, Joel Green, and Marianne Thompson, *Introducing the New Testament: Its Literature and Theology* (Eerdmans 2001, £19.99/$35.00). Pitched at the undergraduate level, but attractively produced, is Delbert Burkett, *An Introduction to the New Testament and the Origins of Christianity* (CUP 2002, £60.00 hb, £22.99

pb/$34.99 pb). The latest edition of Bart D. Ehrman, *The New Testament: A Historical Introduction to the Early Christian Writings* (/OUP 2004, £29.99/2003, $51.95), has a feisty flavor that makes it interesting, but the author is far too impressed by his own skepticism. Ehrman has also produced a more popular version of his own work, viz. *A Brief Introduction to the New Testament* (OUP 2004, £26.99/$44.00).

A more conservative Roman Catholic introduction than that of Raymond Brown (above) is *New Testament Introduction* by Alfred Wikenhauser (op). An alternative evangelical *Introduction to the New Testament* is that of Everett F. Harrison (/Eerdmans 1964, op). The work is far simpler and shorter than those of Guthrie and Carson/Moo, and is now seriously dated. The two volumes by Ralph P. Martin, *New Testament Foundations: A Guide for Christian Students* (Paternoster 1985–86, £15.99 each/Wipf & Stock 2000, $31.00 for the first volume, $45.00 for the second), attempt to mingle traditional questions of introduction, including historical and cultural background, with an emphasis on the theological message of the NT books. The advantage is that it brings together material not normally bound up in one (or two) volumes; the disadvantage is that in some ways the work falls between two stools. Not a few of its judgments belong to the central stream of critical thought. In many ways Martin is the precursor to deSilva (discussed above), who has now eclipsed him.

At opposite ends of the critical spectrum stand two works on critical introduction. Neither owes anything to distinctively "evangelical" tradition, and together they demonstrate how confusing such categories as "liberal" and "conservative" can be. The second edition of *The New Testament: An Introduction* by Norman Perrin and Dennis C. Duling (Harcourt Brace Jovanovich 1982, £16.50 pb/$25.25 pb) fits the NT documents into a doctrinaire history of NT Christianity reconstructed at the beginning of the book. The result is a pretty radical scheme. At the other end stands John A. T. Robinson, *Redating the New Testament* (/TPI nd, op), who argues that all the books in the NT canon were complete before AD 70 and that external ascriptions of authorship in early Christian tradition are remarkably accurate. Both books deserve careful reading by the serious student, if only to discover how data can be made to fit such wildly different schemes.

Quite a number of introductions are cast in somewhat independent molds, as judged by what they add to the discussion of traditional introduction. One of the most helpful to the student is the fairly short book by Bruce M. Metzger, *The New Testament: Background, Growth and Content*, now in its third edition (/Abingdon 2003, $28.00). Somewhat more detailed, and focusing on the factors that produced the NT documents, is C. F. D. Moule, *The Birth of the New Testament* (3rd ed.; Continuum 1981, £19.95/Harper, op). Much more ambitious is the two-volume work by Helmut Koester, *Introduction to the New Testament*, vol. 1: *History, Culture, and Religion of the Hellenistic Age* (2nd ed.; de Gruyter/Aldine 1995, $55.95); vol. 2: *History and Literature of Early Christianity* (2nd ed.; de Gruyter/Aldine 2000, $29.95). The first volume condenses a massive amount of useful material, with only occasional places where another viewpoint might have been desirable (e.g., an overly confident assumption of the pre-Christian roots of full-fledged Gnosticism and a comparatively thin treatment of the Jewish sources). The second volume is extraordinarily tendentious, standing self-consciously in the history-of-religions school as understood by Rudolph Bultmann, to whom the work is dedicated. It is not just that radical positions are taken (e.g., very little is said about Jesus because, like his mentor, Koester feels that there is little the historian can say about him), but that bibliographies are one-sided and extreme positions are put forward as if no other approach to the evidence were possible. For that reason the second volume should not be used by a student just breaking into the problems of NT introduction. A somewhat similar approach is adopted by Christopher Rowland, *Christian Origins: An Account of the Setting and Character of the Most Important Messianic Sect of Judaism* [the American subtitle was *From Messianic Movement to Christian Religion*] (SPCK 1985, £19.99/2nd ed.; Pilgrim Press 2002, $32.00), with results only slightly less radical. Unlike Koester, however, who sees Christianity's roots in the Greco-Roman world, Rowland sees those roots in apocalyptic. The *Introduction to the New Testament* by Charles B. Puskas (/Hendrickson 1989, $24.95) barely addresses traditional questions of introduction, but deals with backgrounds of the NT (Greco-Roman, Jewish, language, text), methods for interpreting the NT (various historical methods, genre criticism), and the formation of early Christianity. Although there is a fair bit of useful material here, Puskas frequently adopts standard critical conclusions as if they were uncontested "givens," so that his work is less valuable than it might have been. Russell Pregeant, *Engaging the New Testament: An Interdisciplinary Introduction* (/Fortress 1997, $38.00 pb), is similarly less interested in traditional historical data regarding the provenance and character of New Testament documents than in approaches to studying them that are driven by new literary criticism and the social sciences. One should mention Raymond F. Collins, *Introduction to the New Testament* (SCM 1992, £17.50 pb/reprint, Galilee Trade 1987, $25.00), which is less concerned with traditional matters of introduction than with the formation and closing of the canon, the use of major literary tools in NT study, and an attempt to reconcile his approach with his own Roman Catholic tradition. Two other substantial introductions are competent middle-of-the-road treatments but have enough eccentricities or awkwardnesses that they do not make it into the first rank: David L. Barr, *New Testament Story: An Introduction* (3rd ed.; Wadsworth 2001, £32.99/$80.95) and Schuyler Brown, *The Origins of Christianity: A Historical Introduction to the New Testament* (/OUP 1993, $35.95 pb). Perhaps what these books unambiguously show is that an "introduction" to the NT now means different things to different people. On bibliographical matters, one should now consult Stanley E. Porter and Lee M. McDonald, *New Testament Introduction* (IBR Bibliographies 12; /Baker 1996, $14.99). The contribution of Carl R. Holladay, *A Critical Introduction to the New Testament: Interpreting the Message and Meaning of Jesus Christ (Expanded CD-ROM Version)* (/Abingdon 2005, $49.00), has as its main goal what is expressed in the subtitle. The work is pitched at the level of the beginning student; its conclusions constitute a fairly conservative liberalism. The CD-ROM provides annotated bibliographies, commentary suggestions, diagrams and illustrations, a full set of endnotes, and an index system that facilitates computer searches.

Perhaps I should mention the spate of books concerned with relating the findings of cultural anthropology and sociology to matters of NT introduction and exegesis. In particular, one thinks of Bruce J.

Malina, *The New Testament World: Insights from Cultural Anthropology* (3rd ed.; SCM 2001, £15.99 pb/Westminster John Knox, $24.95 pb); Wayne A. Meeks, *The First Urban Christians* (2nd ed.; Yale 2003, £14.00 pb/$19.95 pb); and Derek J. Tidball, *An Introduction to the Sociology of the New Testament* (op). In two of the three cases, at least some of the best ideas have been borrowed from the writings of Prof. E. A. Judge, usually published as essays in obscure places.

Finally, there is a plethora of purely popular introductions that will receive no mention here, and of older works that are worth consulting from time to time. The latter include: James Moffatt, *An Introduction to the Literature of the New Testament* (op); A. H. McNeile, *An Introduction to the Study of the New Testament* (op); J. Gresham Machen, *The New Testament: An Introduction to its Literature and History* (reprint, BoT 1976, £7.95/), pitched at a fairly elementary level; and Theodor Zahn's magisterial three-volume *Introduction to the New Testament* (/Kregel nd, $49.95).

2.2 New Testament theologies

In this section I am excluding the myriad of studies that examine only one part of the NT canon—e.g., studies on the theology of Paul, say, or of John. Similarly, I am excluding studies that track one theme right through the canon—as do many of the volumes in the series New Studies in Biblical Theology. I am including only major recent attempts at biblical theology that tackle the entire NT in English—and not all of them. For a survey of the history and central problems in NT theology, one can scarcely do better than begin with Gerhard F. Hasel, *New Testament Theology: Basic Issues in the Current Debate* (/Eerdmans, $25.00 pb). Some of the issues and the bibliography have been updated in my essay on "New Testament Theology," published in *Dictionary of the Later New Testament and Its Developments* (IVP/IVP). For a history of the rise of current critical positions that touch both NT introduction and NT theology, see Stephen Neill, *The Interpretation of the New Testament, 1861–1986*, second edition brought up to date (1961–1986) by N. T. Wright (OUP 1988 pb, £20.99/$35.95), and Werner G. Kümmel, *The New Testament: The History of the Investigation of its Problems* (op). Serious students will want to read William Baird, *History of New Testament Research*. Volume One's subtitle is *From Deism to Tübingen* (/Augsburg Fortress 1992, $58.00); that of Volume Two is *From Jonathan Edwards to Rudolf Bultmann* (/Augsburg Fortress 2002, $40.00). A third volume, *From Biblical Theology to Pluralism*, is forthcoming. A profound though somewhat too skeptical discussion of the nature of NT theology is provided by Robert Morgan, *The Nature of New Testament Theology* (op). An analysis of the challenge of New Testament theology written from an avowedly postmodern perspective is that of A. K. M. Adam, *Making Sense of New Testament Theology: "Modern" Problems and Prospects* (Studies in American Biblical Hermeneutics 11; /Mercer 1995, $26.00). Perhaps the best book-length introduction to the challenges of New Testament theology is the recent volume by Peter Balla, *Challenges to New Testament Theology* (WUNT 95; Mohr Siebeck 1997/Hendrickson 1998, $19.95).

Not to be missed is Andreas Köstenberger's translation of the two-volume set by Adolf Schlatter, *The History of the Christ: The Foundation of New Testament Theology* (/Baker 1997, $39.99) and *The Theology of the Apostles: The Development of New Testament Theology* (/Baker 1998, $39.99). Although Schlatter died in 1938, his work, hitherto available only in German, is richly seminal in a variety of ways. Schlatter was both ahead of his time (anticipating the wiser directions of biblical theology) and behind it (he was openly skeptical of many of the "assured results" of historical criticism). Deeply learned, he nevertheless avoided too much technical interaction, so his work is more accessible than one might suppose.

Several substantial NT theologies have been penned in recent decades by scholars within the evangelical tradition. I shall begin with the older ones. The first, by George Eldon Ladd, *A Theology of the New Testament* (2nd ed.; Eerdmans 1996, £19.99/1993, $36.00), is a comprehensive study that is better on Paul and John than on the Synoptics. Even in the latter, Ladd's treatment of eschatology and salvation history is competent. It is in the failure to distinguish different emphases among the Synoptic Gospels that one could long for more in Ladd's work. The second volume, *New Testament Theology* by Donald Guthrie (IVP 1981, £32.99/IVP 1981, $45.00) is a mammoth volume. Unlike Ladd, who attempts to synthesize the theology of each of the corpora in turn, Guthrie handles theme after theme found in the NT, tracing each theme through each corpus. Perhaps there is not as much synthesis for each theme as one might expect: the price paid for this otherwise attractive format is that the reader finishes his or her study without much of an idea of, say, Paul's distinctive contribution to NT theology as a whole, but with only an idea of his contribution to certain themes. The third effort, Leon Morris's *New Testament Theology* (/Zondervan 1990, $19.99), is much briefer and more elementary, virtues that may commend themselves to those approaching NT theology for the first time. A somewhat different approach is taken in *A Biblical Theology of the New Testament* (/Moody 1994, $34.99), ed. Roy B. Zuck and Darrell L. Bock. Written at the popular level, it is the product of the faculty of Dallas Theological Seminary and reflects, of course, the (sometimes competing) theological predilections of that institution.

Turning to the more recent works, Charles H. H. Scobie, *The Ways of Our God: An Approach to Biblical Theology* (Eerdmans 2003, $45.00), offers not a NT theology but a biblical theology. Working out of a promise-fulfillment framework, Scobie tracks themes through the Bible in an attempt to produce a unified biblical theology. This is the sort of sweeping work that students and pastors love (the writing is highly accessible), while technical scholars tend to say, "Yes, but. . . ." I. Howard Marshall, *New Testament Theology: Many Witnesses, One Gospel* (IVP 2004, £24.99/$40.00), has now effectively eclipsed Ladd's work. Marshall works through the books and corpora of the New Testament in four sections: Jesus, the Synoptics, and Acts; the Pauline letters; the Johannine literature; and the "Catholic" epistles. The introductory essay is an admirable summary of the state-of-play in contemporary biblical theology, with Marshall adjudicating the disputes with admirable good sense. His approach throughout the book is to describe the theology of each New Testament author carefully and then consider "whether the evidence entitles us to speak of a unified theology of the New Testament." Of similar length and stance is the volume by Frank Thielman,

Theology of the New Testament: A Canonical and Synthetic Approach (Zondervan 2005, £20.99/$34.99). He, too, begins with an admirably concise analysis of the state-of-play in the discipline and then divides his material up into three major sections: the Gospels and Acts, the Pauline letters, and the non-Pauline letters and Revelation. A concluding chapter brings the strands together to describe "the theological unity of the New Testament." Thielman habitually avoids entering into the cut and thrust of debate within the discipline of biblical theology, with the result that his book is a better introduction to the actual theological content of the NT documents than to the discipline of biblical theology or to the interface of theology and history—but if one must choose to tilt in one direction or another, this is a better choice than its opposite. Thielman manages to be broadly comprehensive and genuinely edifying—a fine achievement.

The record of major disappointments from the past includes George Barker Stevens, *The Theology of the New Testament* (T&T Clark 1918/ Scribner's 1941, $79.95) and Charles Caldwell Ryrie, *Biblical Theology of the New Testament* (/reprint, Loizeaux Brothers 1996, $14.99; also reprint, ECS Ministries 2005, $14.95 pb).

More broadly, for advanced students the book by James Barr, *The Concept of Biblical Theology: An Old Testament Perspective* (SCM 1999, £30.00/Augsburg Fortress 1999, $48.00), is essential reading despite the "Old Testament" in the title. Barr is far too skeptical about the Bible's unity (see the penetrating review article by Robert W. Yarbrough, "James Barr and the Future of Revelation in History in New Testament Theology," *BBR* 14 [2004]: 105–26), but his evaluations of the discipline are always incisive and he represents something closer to the main stream of thought. More constructive, but with the same canonical sweep, is Brevard S. Childs, *Biblical Theology of the Old and New Testaments: Theological Reflection on the Christian Bible* (SCM 1993, £26.99/Fortress 1993, $47.00). The recently translated *Theology of the New Testament* by Georg Strecker (de Gruyter/Westminster John Knox 2000 [orig. 1996], /$99.90; pb 2001, £35.00/$54.95), represents the best of mainstream German scholarship at the end of the twentieth century. Strecker's six sections treat the theology of Paul, the "tunnel" period, the Synoptics, the Johannine corpus, the "deuteropaulines," and the "Catholic" epistles. Strecker focuses so intently on what is distinctive to each corpus that any sort of broad synthesis is impossible. In other words, by "theology of the New Testament" Strecker is really thinking of the discipline, not the substance, for the substance is in reality theolog*ies* of the New Testament. There is far too little made of Old Testament and Jewish background and far too much of (later) Gnostic sources and ancient Egyptian enthronement ritual. His use of the category of "myth" springs from the Bultmann school. (For a penetrating evaluation of this book, see Simon Gathercole, "Redaction Criticism, Tradition-History and Myth in NT Theology: A Response to Georg Strecker," *Themelios* 28/3 [2003]: 40–48.)

Rudolf Bultmann's *Theology of the New Testament* (in two vols.; only vol. 2 is still available: /Prentice Hall 1970, $42.79) is still worth reading. The work has proved seminal and provocative, and for this reason it is constantly praised. Yet as stimulating as it is, the work is overrated. The very fertility of his ideas is far too often founded on naked antitheses that fly in the face of the evidence, and the beginning student must constantly remember that precisely when Bultmann is at his most quotable he seldom means what the student thinks he does. The reason is that the theological terms have become for Bultmann a set of codes that, stripped of the myths that allegedly adhere to them, convey a shockingly naturalistic existentialism. Hans Conzelmann's *An Outline of the Theology of the New Testament* (op) adheres to the same tradition, but because it was designed to serve as a classroom text it is a little more approachable.

A frequently overlooked but valuable work is that of Ethelbert Stauffer, *New Testament Theology* (op). The book is relatively brief, very condensed, and wisely cautious about the significance of Greco-Roman parallels while reflecting considerable learning in the area. Scarcely less valuable is W. G. Kümmel's *The Theology of the New Testament* (SCM 1976, op). Kümmel focuses on the "major witnesses," i.e., Jesus, Paul, and John, with briefer consideration of other sources. Kümmel finds unity and a strong Lutheran tradition in consistent NT testimony to God's eschatological salvation in Jesus Christ. Better yet is the two-volume work by Leonhard Goppelt, *Theology of the New Testament*, vol. 1: *The Ministry of Jesus in Its Theological Significance*, and vol. 2: *The Variety and Unity of the Apostolic Witness to Christ* (/Eerdmans 1981 and 1983, $32.00 and $35.00 respectively). Goppelt's work is perhaps still the best exposition of a "salvation history" frame of reference to NT interpretation. More difficult to assess, because incomplete, is the *New Testament Theology* of Joachim Jeremias, who managed only one volume, *The Proclamation of Jesus* (SCM 1973, £12.00/Macmillan 1977, $45.00), before his death. Jeremias is at his best in teasing out the significance of the various language forms of Jesus; his work on parables, much praised in former years, has now been superseded. The volume by G. B. Caird, *New Testament Theology*, published posthumously and edited by L. D. Hurst (Clarendon 1994, £62.50 hb, £30.99 pb/$74.00 pb), presents its material in a creative way. Rejecting what he calls the dogmatic approach, the chronological approach, the kerygmatic approach, and the author-by-author approach, Caird proposes "the conference-table approach." To write a New Testament theology is to preside at a conference with all the New Testament authors sitting around the table. The writer presides and engages them in "a colloquium about theological matters that they themselves have put on the agenda." Caird then works through various central themes (e.g., predestination, sin, ethics, eschatology, Christology, and so forth) that are "discussed" by the participants (including Caird, the presider). The work does not belong to the traditional confessional camp, but on many points there is such an exegetical sanity and a fresh way of stating something that the book should be placed very high on anyone's "must read" list. Clever device aside, Caird's work is methodologically much closer to the thematic approach of Guthrie (whom he rather cavalierly dismisses) than he thinks. And of course this approach does scant justice to the entire structure of thought of an individual writer (e.g., Paul). There is little reflection on the relation of the New Testament to the Old.

3

Individual Commentaries

3.1 Synoptics

I am reluctant to include in this little book substantial new sections that introduce divisions of the New Testament (e.g., Synoptics, Johannine corpus, Pauline corpus), lest it become something other than a survey of commentaries. But I cannot forbear to mention four books. Craig L. Blomberg, *Jesus and the Gospels: An Introduction and Survey* (/Broadman & Holman 1997, $34.99), is so eminently sane and readable that it should be on the reading list of anyone who has not perused a serious introduction to the Gospels in some time. The book by Paul Barnett, *Jesus and the Rise of Early Christianity: A History of New Testament Times* (/IVP 1999, $25.00 pb), could have been mentioned at several places in this *Survey*, but I mention it here because it is such a refreshing reversal of many critical presuppositions about the historical Jesus. Here is a scholar who actually sees Jesus to be the wellspring of earliest Christianity: now there's a radical thought. A book edited by Richard Bauckham, *The Gospels for all Christians: Rethinking the Gospel Audiences* (Eerdmans 1998, £14.95 pb/$20.00 pb), nicely challenges a great deal of current critical thinking about the Gospels. The contributing authors present largely convincing evidence that all four Gospels were intended from the beginning to address all Christians, not hermetically sealed sectarian communities. The implications are substantial. Finally, Scot McKnight and Matthew C. Williams have produced *The Synoptic Gospels: An Annotated Bibliography*, one of the IBR Bibliographies (/ Baker 2000, $14.99 pb)—a mine of useful information.

3.2 Matthew

About twenty-five years ago, the Gospel of Matthew did not have many recent, front-rank commentaries elucidating it for students and pastors: pickings were thin. Today, however, the Gospel of Matthew enjoys the support of numerous substantial commentaries. Pride of place should go to the new ICC commentary by *W. D. Davies and Dale C. Allison*. The first volume appeared in 1988 (T&T Clark, £55.00 hb/$39.95 pb), covering introduction and chapters 1–7. The second volume, on Matthew 8–18, was published in 1991 (T&T Clark, £55.00 hb/$39.95 pb), and the third in 1997 (T&T Clark, £55.00 hb/$39.95 pb [the paperback American editions all appeared in 2004]). This work is moderately critical and leaves few stones unturned. Its attention to detail sometimes means the flow of Matthew's argument is less than clear. A one-volume work by the same authors effectively summarizes the content of the three-volume ICC: the title, appropriately, is *Matthew: A Shorter Commentary* (Continuum 2004, £65.00 hb, £19.99 pb/2005, $115.00 hb, $35.00 pb). Scarcely less comprehensive is the commentary by *John Nolland* (NIGTC; 2005, £49.99/$80.00). The introduction is too thin for a work of this sort, but the annotated structural outline of the book is superb and the exegesis of the Greek text more accessible than some other volumes in this series. The two-volume work by *Donald Hagner* in the Word series (1993–1995, £19.99/$39.99 each) tends to be cautious and understated on many points. *Craig Keener* (Eerdmans 1999, £37.99/$65.00—not to be confused with his much shorter IVP volume on Matthew [see below]) has written a massive commentary that in some respects sets new standards. It is engagingly written, and always with the preacher and teacher in mind. Its primary strengths are twofold: first, its unpacking of the socio-historical context of the ancient Mediterranean world, including Jewish-Christian relations; second, its focus on moral lessons. But these very strengths sometimes raise questions: for example, here and there one could argue strenuously against the historical reconstructions Keener adopts. More important, while all recognize that no one commentary can cover everything, Keener's focus on the socio-historical context comes at the expense of penetrating comment on structure, grammar, and sometimes theology. The major German commentary (EKK) by *Ulrich Luz* has now appeared in three English volumes in the Hermeneia series. The three volumes cover, respectively, chapters 1–7 (1989, £27.99/$49.00), chapters 8–20 (2001, £39.99/$69.00), and chapters 21–28 (2005, £49.99/$90.00). The technical scholarship is very good and the translation excellent. But Luz's understanding of who the first readers are—viz. Jewish Christians, which is probably right—leads him to some improbable conclusions about the law in Matthew. One of the strongest features of this commentary is the fairly comprehensive *Wirkungsgeschichte*—the history and reception of the text of Matthew in preceding centuries—connected with each section. For advanced students of Matthew, Luz's commentary is worth the price for that material alone. But the work cannot be the first choice for students and preachers, and not just for reasons of price.

Strictures of price limit the usefulness of the two-volume work by *George Wesley Buchanan* (MBC; 1996–1997, £84.95 for both vols./vol. 1 op, vol. 2 $124.55). Its focus is intertextuality. *Daniel J. Harrington's* SP work (Michael Glazier 1991, £28.50/$41.95) adopts mainstream positions. It is well written, but thinner on theology than one might have expected for a book of this size. *D. A. Carson* in the EBC series (vol. 8, bound with Mark and Luke; /Zondervan 1984—now commonly distributed as two paperback volumes, viz. Matthew 1–12 and Matthew 13–28 respectively; Zondervan, each volume £13.99/$15.99) is larger than the normal parameters allowed for that series and stands within the evangelical tradition. It is now rather dated, but a new and enlarged edition is slated to appear in the next year. Not to be missed is the commentary by *Craig Blomberg* in the NAC series: middle level, and equally good in detail and in the flow of the argument (/1992, $29.99).

A shorter but useful commentary within the evangelical tradition is that of *Robert H. Mounce* (NIBC; 1995, £5.00 pb/1991, $14.95 pb). Pitched at about the same level, roughly mainstream in its theological orientation but full of condensed and insightful exegesis, is *Robert H. Smith* (ACNT; 1989, $23.00 pb). The TNTC commentary by *R. T. France* (1986, £11.99/1987, $15.00) is outstanding, although not many will follow him in his interpretation of the eschatological discourse.

Other substantial commentaries from the past two decades or so, each slightly off the beaten track, include the following. *Robert H. Gundry* (Eerdmans, $39.50) is the most rigorously redaction-critical commentary on Matthew yet to appear. It detects a "midrashic" approach to the Jesus tradition at many points, although without ever telling us whence the definition and formal characteristics of midrash are derived. Gundry has chosen to interact with few secondary sources. Few preachers will find it serviceable in sermon preparation. The commentary by *Francis W. Beare* (/Harper 1982, op) is more traditional in its layout but rather skeptical in many of its historical judgments. Worse, its bibliography and discussion were at least fifteen years out of date the day the work was published. *Daniel Patte* (Continuum 1996 [though a reprint of 1986], £19.99/Fortress 1986, $28.95 pb) shows his interest in his subtitle: *A Structural Commentary on Matthew's Faith*. Frederick Dale Bruner has produced two volumes in which, again, the subtitle helps to explain the author's purpose: *The Christbook: A Historical/Theological Commentary*, vol. 1: *Matthew 1–12*; vol. 2: *Matthew 13–28*. A new edition has appeared (2004, vol. 1, Crossroad, £25.99/Eerdmans, $45.00; vol. 2, Eerdmans, £28.99/$50.00). Despite a substantial amount of useful theological discussion, the work can be challenged rather frequently at the exegetical level. *Margaret Davies* (JSOT, £34.33 hb or £17.07 pb/$57.50 hb or $29.95 pb) offers a rather slender reader-response approach to Matthew. The commentary of *David E. Garland* (Crossroad, £15.67/$27.50 hb or $22.00 pb) is not much longer but focuses on a broader array of literary and to some extent theological issues. Samuel Tobias Lachs has written *A Rabbinic Commentary on the New Testament: The Gospels of Matthew, Mark, and Luke* (/Ktav 1987, $39.50 hb or $25.00 pb). J. Enoch Powell, *The Evolution of the Gospel: A New Translation of the First Gospel with*

Commentary and Introductory Essay (Yale 1994, £25.00/$45.00), is a highly idiosyncratic treatment of the Gospel, including an introductory essay in defense of the priority of Matthew and of the thesis that Mark and Luke had no other sources.

Before turning to more commentaries, I should mention several books that, while not commentaries, have special value for the study of Matthew. The first, a brief volume edited by Graham Stanton, *The Interpretation of Matthew* (IRT), first appeared in 1983, was for a while op, but is now back in print (£25.00/$29.95). It offers a useful compendium of scholarship up to the time of writing. More important is Graham Stanton's own work, *A Gospel for a New People: Studies in Matthew*, a volume loaded with informed and judicious comment even where one may want to disagree. The hardback edition (T&T Clark 1991/1992) is permanently out of print, but the work was reprinted in paperback by another publisher (/Westminster John Knox 1994, $27.95). The book by R. T. France, *Matthew: Evangelist and Teacher* (Paternoster 1989, £9.99/Zondervan 1990, $19.99), is well written and judicious on both critical and theological issues; it is an able introduction to the study of Matthew, even though it is now a decade and a half old. More recent, but less controlled by the text, are Warren Carter, *Matthew: Storyteller, Interpreter, Evangelist* (Hendrickson 2004, $19.95) and Howard Clarke, *The Gospel of Matthew and Its Readers: A Historical Introduction to the First Gospel* (Indiana University 2003, $55.00). The latter includes many reflections on how this Gospel has been used (and abused!) in the past. Beyond these volumes, of course, are many monographs that receive no notice here.

One of the standard middle-level commentaries is that of *David Hill* (NCB; 1981, op). The introduction is useful, and the commentary itself is a model of compression; but its most helpful remarks are usually a digested (and not always acknowledged) form of P. Bonnard, *Evangile selon S. Matthieu* (CNT)—still one of the best treatments of Matthew for the student or pastor who can read French (especially in the 2nd ed., 1970). *Douglas R. A. Hare* has written the entry for the Interpretation series (Westminster John Knox, £20.00/$29.95). The contribution of *Craig S. Keener* to the IVPNTC series (/IVP, $25.00) is eminently accessible and responsible, and could fruitfully be given to lay leaders, while those better trained could skip this one and read Keener's more substantial work (above). An accessible commentary that studies Matthew through an array of approaches—literary, historical, theological—is that of *Donald Senior* (ANTC; 1998, £14.99/$25.00). The IBT volume by the same author (/1997, $20.00) is a masterful survey of modern scholarship, not a commentary. *W. Hendriksen* (/Baker 1973, $49.99) is verbose, preachy, and not always acquainted with discussions current when he wrote, but his obvious love for Scripture and concern to expound the text make him a useful if stodgy guide for the preacher who will wade through him. Give a miss to *John J. Kilgallen* (MBC; 1992, £69.95/$109.95). The exegesis is thin anyway, but at this price (for 348 pp.) one would either have to be stupid or as rich as Croesus to consider it. *H. Benedict Green* (NClar; 1975, op) is very concise and reveals an excellent knowledge of OT and rabbinic background. Although provocative and often stimulating, it tends toward viewpoints characterized by eccentric independence. The commentary by *C. S. Mann and W. F. Albright* (AB; 1971, $37.50 hb; 1995, $39.95 pb) is highly uneven, a poor representative of the series. They have put together a substantial introduction, but the commentary itself is very thin. *Leon Morris* in the Pillar series (Eerdmans, £28.99/$47.00) is very much in the tradition we have come to expect from him: workmanlike, conservative, and generally helpful, but the quality of interaction varies quite a bit for a commentary of such length.

The spate of redaction-critical or special thematic studies on Matthew has slowed down, eclipsed by other interests. The following sample does not include the most recent, but I have chosen them largely because they are still constantly referred to in the literature and/or belong pretty closely to the commentary genre. The approaches of Bornkamm, Held, Strecker, and Trilling are summarized in J. Rohde, *Rediscovering the Teaching of the Evangelists* (op). At a simple level, *Wolfgang Trilling* (NTSR; Sheed & Ward 1978, £7.50 pb/Crossroad 1981, $4.95), a Roman Catholic scholar, attempts to combine redaction-critical findings on Matthew with spiritual application. *E. Schweizer* (/Westminster John Knox 1975, $29.95) is really an extension of his Mark commentary (below): indeed, in this volume Schweizer devotes almost all of his space to non-Markan material in Matthew, making the work almost useless to those who do not have the other commentary. His source-critical theories and related *Sitze im Leben* are not likely to command wide assent, but those theological comments that do not depend on his overarching reconstruction are often astute. *Paul Minear* (/Pilgrim Press 1982, op) has provided a brief redaction-critical commentary focusing on the structure of the book and concluding that the first Gospel was originally intended as a manual for adult education in the early church. *J. D. Kingsbury*, author of a much-cited redaction-critical study of Matthew (*Matthew: Structure, Christology, Kingdom*), has written the brief (128 pp.) ProcC work (rev. ed.; 1981, op). Few will be persuaded of the overriding importance of the Son of God title, and the work is too short to be of sustained use. Although many books on Matthew's use of the Old Testament have appeared, the seminal one in recent discussion has been that of Krister Stendahl, *The School of St. Matthew and Its Use of the Old Testament*, and it is good to see it kept in print (/Sigler 1991, $25.00 hb or $18.00 pb). Finally, one should perhaps mention the work of Donald Senior, *The Passion of Jesus in the Gospel of Matthew* (/Liturgical 1985, $14.95). Considering the reputation of the author, earned because of his very substantial contributions elsewhere, the commentary by *Rudolf Schnackenburg* (Eerdmans 2002, £13.99 pb/$24.00 pb) is a disappointment. The contribution by *Russell Pregeant* (/CCT; 2004, $24.99) is little interested in the historical context of either Jesus or Matthew but rather in the interplay between Matthew's story and the contemporary reader.

Old standards, a few of them recently reprinted, include *J. A. Broadus* (/Kregel [1886] 1990, $26.99 pb), which still retains some value for the preacher (although his handling of OT texts within Matthew is generally appalling), and *A. H. McNeile* on the Greek text—originally published in 1915 but now regrettably op. *A. Plummer* (1915, op) is patchy but occasionally helpful, especially in the sequence of thought. C. H. Spurgeon's exposition of Matthew originally bore the title *The Gospel of the Kingdom*, but it has recently been reprinted under the title *The Gospel of Matthew* (/Fleming Revell 1995, $21.99 hb), and can be suggestive to the preacher, but it should be used only in conjunction with a modern scholarly commentary. *Joseph Addison Alexander* is still op. *G. H. Morrison* (/AMG, in three paperback vols., op) was a Scot whose 1928 exposition is on various verses in Matthew rather than a comprehensive treatment. *David Thomas* (orig. 1873) is again out of print.

Among the shorter or more popular works, the two short volumes by *N. T. Wright*, covering Matthew 1–15 and Matthew 16–28 respectively (SPCK 2002, £8.99 per vol./Westminster John Knox 2004, $14.95 per vol.), are written with color and verve. Wright puts so much weight on the theme of Jesus bringing the exile to an end that other themes of equal or greater importance are often lost to view, generating a feeling that the work is an exercise in brilliant reductionism. The BST contribution is by *Michael Green* and is worth a quick skim (2001, £9.99/$16.00). *F. V. Filson* (Black 1971, op) is only moderately useful. *R. V. G. Tasker* (TNTC; op) is well written but too brief to be of much value, and in any case it has now been superseded by R. T. France's replacement volume for the series (above). *G. E. P. Cox* (TBC; op) suffers much from lack of space; *J. Fenton* (Pelican; 1964, op) packs more into his pages but is very uneven in relation to the needs of the preacher. It varies from the very useful to the very disappointing. *K. Stendahl* in the New Peake uses small space with greater profit and is often worth consulting. Other popular commentaries on Matthew, all of them fairly recent, include: *Myron S. Augsburger* (CC; 1987, £12.99 hb/$24.99 hb or 1989, $9.99 pb), *Peter F. Ellis* (Liturgical 1986, £5.50/1985, op), Michael B. Green (Hodder 1988, op/Word 1989, $9.99), *Daniel J. Harrington* (/Liturgical 1985, £4.50/1983, $4.95), *Miriam Perlewitz* (MBS; Glazier 1991, £11.99 pb/Liturgical 1988, $16.95 hb or $12.95 pb), *William G. Thompson* (Paulist 1989, op), *G. Jerome Albrecht and Michael J. Albrecht* (PBC; Concordia 2001, $12.99), *Bruce B. Barton* in the LABC (/Tyndale 1996, $16.99), *Ivor H. Jones* (Epworth 1994, £9.99/TPI, $14.95), *Lawrence E. Glasscock* (/Moody 1997, $23.99), *Thomas G. Long* in the WBComp (/Westminster John Knox 1997, $27.95), and the slender and skeptical guide of *John Riches* in NTG (JSOT, op/SAP 1996, $17.95). D. A. Carson attempts to move from text to sermon in *When Jesus Confronts the World: An Exposition of Matthew*

8–10 (reprint, Paternoster 1995, £1.99 pb/Baker 1987, op). Although this book and his *Sermon on the Mount* are both op with Baker, they have been combined into one volume and in that form they remain in print with that publisher (/1999, $19.99). D. A. Carson, *God with Us* (/JKO 1995, np) is a brief commentary on Matthew designed for home Bible studies and adult Sunday School classes.

Past disappointments include *W. C. Allen* (ICC; 1922, £45.00/), *B. T. D. Smith* (CGT; 1927, op), *Theodore Robinson* (Moffatt; 1947, op), and *J. F. Walvoord* (/Moody 1974, op). A hybrid difficult to classify—part commentary, part expository sermon—is the work of *John MacArthur* in 4 vols. (/Moody 1985–89, £14.99/$21.99 per vol.). These books are wordy and often betray too little time and care taken with the text, so that they cannot be read as reliable commentary; but the amount of information goes beyond that of most expositions. Doubtless they will well serve the well-read layperson and the poorly trained preacher.

No serious treatment of the Sermon on the Mount can afford to ignore Robert A. Guelich, *The Sermon on the Mount: A Foundation for Understanding* (Word 1991, op/$16.99), which in many respects supersedes W. D. Davies, *The Setting of the Sermon on the Mount* (CUP 1966, op/$10.95; now reprinted, Scholars 1989, in the Brown Judaic Series). Advanced studies include Hans Dieter Betz, *Essays on the Sermon on the Mount* (/Fortress 1985, $12.95). This early work by Betz has now in any case been eclipsed by his *The Sermon on the Mount: A Commentary on the Sermon on the Mount, Including the Sermon on the Plain*—a 695-page work that gives more weight to ostensible Greco-Roman parallels than they deserve (/Fortress 1995, $79.00). More useful for the preacher, though far too atomistic in its approach, is Georg Strecker, *The Sermon on the Mount: An Exegetical Commentary* (T&T Clark 1988, £13.95/ Abingdon 1988, $14.00). Carl G. Vaught, *The Sermon on the Mount: A Theological Interpretation* (Baylor University 2001, £18.50/$24.95) is worth scanning; the works by Oscar Stephen Brooks, *The Sermon on the Mount: Authentic Human Values* (UPA 1985, op), and Sjef van Tilborg, *The Sermon on the Mount as an Ideological Intervention: A Reconstruction of Meaning* (Van Gorcum 1986, $30.00), in their effort to be relevant, end up domesticating the text in service to extra-biblical ideology. Several monographs on the Sermon on the Mount appear every year, but I cannot forbear to mention one more: Charles H. Talbert, *Reading the Sermon on the Mount: Character Formation and Decision Making in Matthew 5–7* (University of South Carolina 2004, $29.95; Baker 2006, $17.99). The reflection is painfully divorced from the historical Jesus: one marvels at how bright Matthew is and how unknown Jesus is. Yet the work stimulates reflection of many kinds and is worth close reading.

Useful popular expositions of the Sermon on the Mount include *D. M. Lloyd-Jones* (IVP 1976, £18.99/Eerdmans 1984, $29.00); *D. A. Carson* (Paternoster 1999, £1.99/Baker is op, but has just brought out an edition bound with *When Jesus Confronts the World* [see above]); C. H. Dodd, *Gospel and Law* (1951, op); *Archibald M. Hunter* (1966, op); J. R. W. Stott, *Christian Counter-Culture* (BST; IVP 1984, £9.99/IVP 1988, $15.00); *Jan Lambrecht* (/Liturgical 1985, $12.95 pb); and Dennis Hamm, *The Beatitudes in Context: What Luke and Matthew Meant* (/Liturgical 1990, $7.95). The subtitles of the next two entries disclose the respective focus of each: Roland H. Worth Jr., *The Sermon on the Mount: Its Old Testament Roots* (Paulist 1997, £20.75/$22.95), argues that all of the antitheses find their roots in Torah; and Dale Allison, *The Sermon on the Mount: Inspiring the Moral Imagination* (Crossroad 1999, £9.99 pb/$17.95).

3.3 Mark

For pastors, the best five commentaries on Mark are by *R. T. France* (NIGTC; 2002, £39.99/$58.00), *James Edwards* (Pillar; 2001, £22.00/$41.95), *William Lane* (2nd ed.; NIC; 1995, £25.99/$45.00), *Morna D. Hooker* (BNTC/HNTC; 1993, op/$29.95), and *James Brooks* (NAC; 1991, /$29.99). The first, on the Greek text, is nevertheless remarkably accessible and includes a healthy mix of history, theology, social context, even warmth. The second, by Edwards, is less daunting for those with little Greek, but is demonstrably the fruit of years of work on this Gospel. Lane's demands that the reader know Greek only while reading the footnotes; it is slightly more dated. Hooker's work is invariably competent, though sometimes she is more skeptical than she needs to be about the authenticity of Jesus' words and deeds, and she maintains her increasingly improbable reading of Mark 10:45. Brooks is workmanlike.

Two others should be appended to this initial list of five: *C. E. B. Cranfield* (CUP 1959, £22.99 pb/$34.99 pb) is now very dated, but it says something for the quality of his work and the reverent and understated nature of his prose that this relatively short commentary on the Greek text is still in print. *C. S. Mann* (AB; 1986, /$44.95), though it is a major contribution, tends to focus on words and structure at the expense of theology.

None of this is to say that these seven are the most detailed English-language commentaries on Mark. That prize must be shared by several other works. The first volume on Mark in the WBC series was by *Robert A. Guelich* (on 1:1–8:26; 1989, £19.99/$39.99). It is extraordinarily detailed, though sometimes incautiously speculative in its recreation of the church circumstances Mark allegedly addresses. Guelich's untimely death meant that the second volume was passed on to *Craig Evans* (on 8:27–16:20; 2001, £19.99/$39.99). It is stronger on technical issues than on the theology of the book. The massive (1,296 pp.) commentary on Mark by *Robert H. Gundry* (/Eerdmans 1992, $60.00; more recently this work has been published in two volumes, on Mark 1–8 and Mark 9–16 respectively, both appearing in 2000: vol. 1, $40.00; vol. 2, $50.00) is more conservative and is packed with endless interaction with other scholars. But with single-eyed determination Gundry pursues a thematic center that few scholars find as determinative for Mark as he does. The work of *Joel Marcus* (AB; vol. 1 on Mark 1–8; Doubleday 2000, £35.00/$42.50) is still incomplete. What has appeared so far is technically of the first rank, but it is far too skeptical regarding what can be known about the historical Jesus. Mark emerges as a late Paulinist.

Several other recent commentaries deserve mention. *Ben Witherington III* has produced a commentary focusing (as is customary for him) on the socio-rhetorical features of Mark (/Eerdmans 2001, £19.99/$35.00). He is always worth reading, so long as he is read in conjunction with one or two other commentaries that aim at more rounded coverage. *Sharyn Dowd* calls her work "a literary and theological commentary," and so it is (/Smyth and Helwys 2000, $19.00), but it is too brief to stand among the major contributions. The same must be said for *Edwin K. Broadhead* in the Readings series (SAP 2001, £55.00 hb or £22.50 pb/$110.00 hb or $44.95 pb)—to say nothing of the outrageous price. *John R. Donahue* (SP; 2002, £18.15/$41.95) is a substantial contribution of almost five hundred pages, but it focuses a bit narrowly on "intratextuality" (reading Mark as Mark and by Mark, examining all the literary figures and structures, etc.) and "intertextuality" (how the text relates to other streams of tradition). In other words, like Witherington if for different reasons, this is a fine supplementary commentary.

Two other major commentaries, though now dated, are *H. B. Swete* (reprint, /Kregel 1978, $25.99), which is dull and stodgy in spite of its thorough scholarship, and *Vincent Taylor* (2nd ed.; Macmillan 1982, £95.00/op), which was the first major commentary on Mark in English to utilize a restrained form-criticism. For a reprint, it is outrageously priced.

Hugh Anderson (NCB; revised pb edition 1981 op/$18.00) offers a sane presentation of Mark's theological understanding of Jesus, avoiding the extreme subtleties found in some specialized recent treatments, yet stands painfully loose on the historical reliability of Mark. *E. Schweizer* (/Westminster John Knox 1970, $39.95) incorporates insight from early redactional study, sometimes with considerable profit. *Sherman Johnson* (BNTC/HNTC; reprint, /Hendrickson 1987, op), which preceded the Hooker volume (above) in this series, is disappointing in relation to the needs of the preacher. *A. M. Hunter*'s commentary (TBC; 1969, op) does not live up to his usual standards. *C. F. D. Moule* (CBC; 1965, £14.99 pb/$20.99 pb) packs many helpful comments into a small space, but the space is so small that the book cannot claim first priority. *Alan Cole*'s TNTC commentary has appeared in a revised edition (1990, £9.99/1989, $14.00). It is certainly worth careful reading, but cannot, of course, compete with the major works. *C. L. Mitton* (Epworth 1957, op) offers many practical points of help to the preacher but is both dated and hard to come by. *Dennis E. Nineham* (Pelican; 1969/1964, op) is stimulating but occasionally irritating owing to a penchant to read behind the passage rather than the passage itself, and sometimes to read in defiance of the passage. *Larry Hurtado's* 1983 GNC commentary has metamorphosed into its NIBC form (Paternoster 1989, £11.99/Hendrickson 1995, $14.95). It is a moderately redaction-critical commentary that will serve pastors well when used in conjunction with France or Edwards.

Among older works, *A. E. J. Rawlinson* (op) can sometimes be picked up secondhand. *Joseph Alexander* was in print for a while (BoT/Kregel) but is again out of print.

Useful tools include Ralph P. Martin, *Mark: Evangelist and Theologian* (Paternoster 1979/Zondervan 1986, op), which is not a commentary but a (now somewhat dated) study of the background and theology of Mark as treated in contemporary scholarship up to the late 1970s. The contemporary equivalents are Francis J. Moloney, *Mark: Storyteller, Interpreter, and Evangelist* (/Hendrickson 2004, $19.94), and Donald H. Juel, *The Gospel of Mark* (IBT; 1999, /$20.00). Frank J. Matera, *What Are They Saying about Mark?* (Paulist 1987, op), is both too dated and too short to be useful. Etienne Trocmé, *The Formation of the Gospel according to Mark* (1975, op), is not really a commentary but an exposition of Trocmé's mildly eccentric but always stimulating views on the Gospel's development. Two other works that are not commentaries but that contribute substantially to our understanding are Martin Hengel, *Studies in the Gospel of Mark* (/reprint, Wipf & Stock 2003, $25.00), and Ernest Best, *Mark: The Gospel as Story* (T&T Clark 1988, op/$29.95 hb or $27.95 pb). Bas van Iersel, *Reading Mark* (T&T Clark 1989, op/Liturgical 1989, $14.95), the ET of a work that originally appeared in Dutch, makes literary criticism comprehensible to the general reader. It includes many useful insights and is worth a good, fast read. M. D. Hooker's *The Message of Mark* (Epworth 1983, £6.95/TPI 1983, op) covers much in few words.

Among commentaries that are not quite ordinary commentaries—*caveat emptor*—I should mention five. The focus of three of them is disclosed in their respective subtitles: Ole Davidson, *The Narrative Jesus: A Semiotic Reading of Mark's Gospel* (/Århus University Press 1993, $39.95); John Paul Heil, *The Gospel of Mark as Model for Action: A Reader-Response Commentary* (reprint, /Wipf & Stock 2001, $39.00); and Bas

M. F. van Iersel, *Mark: A Reader-Response Commentary* (SAP 1998, £70.00/$140.00). The fourth is a fresh presentation of Augustine on Mark: Michael Cahill, trans. and ed., *The First Commentary on Mark: An Annotated Translation* (OUP 1998, £37.00/$52.00). And finally, the ACCS volume on Mark is by *Thomas C. Oden and Christopher A. Hill* (/IVP 1998, £35.00/$40.00).

W. Hendriksen on Mark (/Baker 1975, $44.99) is not as good as on Matthew. *Walter W. Wessel* (EBC vol. 8, bound with Matthew [see above]; or available as a separate paperback, Zondervan 1995, £9.99/$16.99) makes reasonable use of small space but without much interaction with secondary literature. The new EBC should be out within a year or so. *David E. Garland* has provided the volume for the NIVAC series (Zondervan 1996, £17.99/$29.99). Now in a revised edition, *P. J. Achtemeier* (ProcC; reprint, Wipf & Stock 2004, $18.00), makes too much of the church crisis in the sixties AD and too little of the historical Jesus.

Mark's Gospel seems to be a favorite among those who produce popular or shorter commentaries. Among these treatments, *Johnnie C. Godwin* (LBBC; Broadman 1979, $11.99), *Terence J. Keegan* (Paulist 1981, op), *John J. Kilgallen* (Paulist 1989, op), and *Ralph P. Martin* (KPG; 1986/1981, op/$15.00) are responsible surveys of their kind. *Allen Black* (/College Press 1995, $29.99) is very accessible and full of good sense but is aimed rather more at the lay reader than at the serious student or preacher. *Elliott C. Maloney* (Continuum 2002, £11.99/$19.00) briefly expounds the Gospel in such a way as to argue that the kingdom is in the hearts of human beings. *R. Kent Hughes* (/Crossway 1989, 2 vols., $14.95 each) is more sermonic but one of the best in that genre. Other popular treatments include *Karen A. Barta* (MBS; 1991, £11.50 pb/1988, $13.95 hb or $12.95 pb), *Paul R. McReynolds* (/Standard 1989, $11.95), *Ivor Powell* (/Kregel 1986, $17.99 pb), *Michael Wilcock* (/CLC 1983, op), *Louis Barbieri* (/Moody 1995, $23.99), *Bruce B. Barton* (/Tyndale House Publishers 1994, $16.99), *Phillip J. Cunningham* (Paulist 1995, op/$10.95), *Douglas R. A. Hare* (WBComp; 1996, £12.99 /$24.95), *Hugh M. Humphrey* (Paulist 1992, £10.99/$11.95), *Denis McBride* (Dominican Publications 1996, £8.99/), *Sidney Poe* (/Word Aflame Press 1994, $12.99), and, in the respected BST series, *Donald English*

(1992, £9.99/$15.00). The short work by *William R. Telford* in the NTG series (just taken over by Continuum 2003, £8.99/2004, $16.94) is of a higher order but too brief to be of much use to the preacher. *D. Edmond Hiebert* (/Bob Jones Univ. Press 1994, $23.95) has the length of a major commentary (516 pp.), is characterized by the gentleness and conservative devotion for which its author is well known, but lacks both bite and contemporary engagement. The book by Frederick Neumann, *The Binding Truth: A Selective Homiletical Commentary on the New Testament*, vol. 2: *Why Are You Afraid? The Gospels of Mark and John* (/Pickwick 1984, op) is so odd I am uncertain why it was published. Neumann died in 1967. This is posthumously published sermonic material with useful nuggets but no structure and an English style that is not easy to read. *R. T. France* has written a little commentary on Mark (Bible Reading Fellowship 1996, £8.99/), but most readers of this *Survey* will much prefer his NIGTC volume (above). The entry to the FoB series is *Geoffrey Grogan* (Christian Focus Publications, £6.99/), but this volume is characterized more by doctrinal awareness than by close attentiveness to the text. Worth perusing is *Mark Horne* (/Canon Press 2003, $14.00), a devotional work that also tries to show the outworkings of OT typology in Jesus as he fulfills and redefines the kingdom.

3.4 Luke

The Gospel of Luke is now well served by several major commentaries. Pride of place goes to the two volumes of *Darrell L. Bock* (/BECNT; 1994–96, $109.98 for the pair or $54.99 each). It is recent, comprehensive, well written, and intelligent. If you buy this pair by Bock, you do not need the other two commentaries on Luke that he has written (see below). Almost as good, but now more dated, is the commentary by *Joseph A. Fitzmyer* (AB; 2 vols., 1981 and 1985, $55.00 each). The work is a masterpiece of learning, and written with clarity and verve. Not all will be persuaded by the author's positions on dating, sources, and details of historicity, but there are few questions Fitzmyer has not thought deeply about, and his competence in the Semitic parallels informs his work throughout. No less learned is the large

commentary by *I. Howard Marshall* (NIGTC; 1978, £24.99/$55.00).
Unfortunately the prose is so densely packed, owing not least to the
fact that the notes are incorporated into the text, that some will make
heavy weather of it. Moreover, it presupposes reasonable proficiency
in the Greek text. Those with the requisite skills will benefit greatly
from reading it.

Joel Green has filled in the lacuna in the NIC series (1997, $52.00)
with a commentary of almost one thousand pages. It is full of thoughtful interaction with contemporary scholarship, but I do not think it is
either as rigorous or as accurate as the work of Bock. Its forte is narrative
historiography or discourse analysis. At times it reads like a series of
essays, and occasionally it is a bit difficult for the user to discover just
what Green says on particular points. Indeed, Green's almost exclusively
literary reading means (for instance) that he ignores discussion about
the relation between Luke and the other Synoptics, including the major
historical issues implicit in such discussions. Occasionally he sidles into
sociological considerations, but otherwise his literary reading controls
the agenda and makes even this very large commentary seem narrow,
confining, and sometimes skewed. *John Nolland* (WBC; 3 vols.; Word,
£19.99/$39.99 each) seems a bit bland after Bock, Fitzmyer, and Green,
and suffers from the inefficient WBC format, but he is certainly more
balanced than Green in the range of approaches he entertains. Another major commentary (933 pp.) is the work of *C. F. Evans* (TPINT;
1990, op). Theologically it stands in a far more skeptical tradition than
either Marshall or Fitzmyer and rarely interacts with literature and
positions of a more centrist (let alone conservative) stance. For those
who want to become informed of how Christians in the patristic period
read Mark, help is at hand from *Arthur A. Just Jr.*, ed. (ACCS; 2003,
£28.99/$40.00).

For those who read German or French, the massive work of François
Bovon is as rich on technical points as any of the above and is sometimes more seminal in the theological arena. Three of the projected four
volumes have appeared in German (EKK) and French (CNT); the first
volume, on Luke 1:1–9:50, has appeared in English in the Hermeneia
series (2002, $59.00).

There are many other important commentaries on Luke that are substantial without being gargantuan. *Luke Timothy Johnson* (SP; 1992, £26.99/$29.95) is above all a work of literary analysis. It tends not to take up issues of, say, the origin of a pericope or development of ideas or tradition before the text as it stands. It devotes quite a bit of space to literary analogies in the ancient world. Robert C. Tannehill, *The Narrative Unity of Luke-Acts: A Literary Interpretation*, vol. 1: *The Gospel According to Luke* (2nd ed.; Fortress 1990, £12.99 pb/$22.00 pb) writes with similar interests at heart. *David L. Tiede* (ACNT; 1991, £10.99 pb/1989, $17.25 pb) is a nontechnical commentary that adopts more or less standard positions. Written in a condensed style, this commentary assumes that most of Luke's stances reflect considerably later Christianity rather than its ostensible subject. *Darrell L. Bock*'s entry to the NIVAC series is one of the stronger volumes (1996, £27.99/$29.99). If you possess either this volume or his BECNT volumes on Luke (see above), you can skip his IVPNTC on Luke (1994, £9.99/$22.00). A conservative Lutheran perspective is brought to us in two volumes by *Arthur A. Just Jr.* (/Concordia; vol. 1 on 1:1–9:50, 1996; vol. 2 on 9:51–24:53, 1997; $42.99 each). See also his important work in the ACCS series, above. *Robert H. Stein* (NAC; 1992, $29.99) is good value for the money, more so than *Robert C. Tannehill* (ANTC; £16.99/$28.00), which seems a bit tired after his larger work (see above). Like his earlier volume, Tannehill is more interested in inferring the cultural and social realities in which the text was ostensibly read than in probing very deeply into the text itself. *Craig A. Evans* has provided the Luke commentary for NIBC (1995, £5.00 pb/$27.95). It is tightly written and strong on the technicalities of Old Testament and Jewish antecedents. The commentary by *David Gooding* (IVP/Eerdmans 1987, op) focuses attention on the text, especially its flow, but does not interact with other literature. It is a fine way for the serious general reader to get into the text of Luke.

E. E. Ellis (NCB; 1981, op) contains valuable material, especially on the background and purposes of passages and on the flow of the argument, but can be frustrating on particular verses. Similarly, *G. B. Caird* (Pelican; Penguin 1990, op/Viking Penguin 1964, $10.00) is good value for the money, although comments can be thin on the details. The series aim is not to provide material that is technical or devotional but simply "to bring out the meaning the Evangelists intended to convey to their original readers." *A. R. C. Leaney* (BNTC; 1985/HNTC; 1987, op) also tends to be thin where one most hopes for help. *Fred B. Craddock* (Interpretation; 1990, £20.00/$29.95) is helpful to the preacher who has done his serious exegesis by resorting to more technical commentaries. *Judith Lieu* (Epworth 1997, /$14.95) is crystal clear as to what Lieu thinks but less clear as to what Luke thinks. *J. M. Creed* (Macmillan 1942, op) is better but decisively belongs to pre-war scholarship. *Marvin C. Pate* (Moody 1995, £14.99/$23.99) has written a work that is workmanlike, warm, accessible, and without too many technicalities. The series constraints on both *Sharon H. Ringe* (WBComp; 1995, /$24.95) and C. M. Tuckett (NTG; 1996, £10.99/) make them of little use as commentaries for students and preachers. Perhaps Ringe is worth a fast skim after a student has done more detailed work, for although she skips the details she is constantly trying to listen to how each unit fits into the Gospel of Luke as a whole. *G. H. P. Thompson* (NClar; 1972, op) is a moderately useful and fairly conservative commentary, but it is severely restricted by lack of space; *Victor Prange* (2nd ed.; /Concordia 2005, $14.99) is more conservative but also fairly limited. *A. Plummer* (ICC; 4th ed.; 1901, £45.00/op) was once good, but its reputation lingers on after later writers have superseded the work. *W. Manson* did himself less than justice in the Moffatt series (1930, op). *E. Tinsley* (CBC; 1965, £19.99/$31.99) is occasionally useful over and above the larger commentaries, but skip it unless the book can be borrowed. F. Danker, *Jesus and the New Age According to St Luke* (Fortress 1987, op), is of some value to the scholar and the layperson, but the heart of his argument reappears in his little ProcC work (1987, op). *W. R. F. Browning* (TBC; 1982, op) is surprisingly good but too brief to be of primary importance. *Leon Morris* (TNTC; revised ed., 1988, £9.99/$15.00) is good value for the money, one of the better volumes in the series—even if occasionally the constraints of the series means he skates over some difficult questions and skirts some contemporary issues. Something similar should be said with respect to *Mark C. Black* (/College Press 1996, $32.99). *R. Summers* (/Word 1972) and *W. J. Harrington* (/Newman 1967) are both out of print. *Michael Wilcock* (BST; 3rd ed.; 1997, £9.99/$15.00) provides some excellent grist for the preacher's mill, provided he is used in conjunction with a major commentary. *Walter L. Liefeld* (EBC vol. 8, bound with Matthew and Mark, above; available as a separate paperback, Zondervan, $17.99) packs a great deal of astute comment into relatively small compass. In still smaller compass, but with less astuteness, *Robert J. Karris* (/Doubleday 1977, op) offers a brief commentary based on the Jerusalem Bible. *Robert E. Obach* and *Albert Kirk* (Paulist 1986, op) is worth a glance, as is *Philip van Linden* (MBS; 1991, £11.50 pb/1986, op). *Lewis Foster* (/Standard 1986, $12.99) is not worth even that. R. E. O. White, *Luke's Case for Christianity* (Bible Reading Fellowship 1987, op/Morehouse 1990, $6.95) is the sort of thing to put into the hand of the layperson just beginning to do some serious Bible reading.

From the preacher's point of view, *J. Norval Geldenhuys* (the inaugural volume in NIC; 1971 [orig. 1951], /$27.99—replaced by Joel Green, above) has now so far been eclipsed that it is not even worth skimming. Worth a fast skim is the old two-volume commentary by *F. Godet* (reprint, Wipf & Stock 2004, 2 vols., $48.00 each). Godet is virtually pre-critical but can be valuable. Apart from his digressions on old and forgotten controversies, he is consistently clear and to the point. He is still worth using in conjunction with a more recent work. Useful in the same sorts of ways is *William Hendriksen* (NTC; 1979, £15.95/1978, $29.95). A fine expository model is found in *R. Kent Hughes* (/Crossway 1998, $24.99). *Henry Wansbrough* (/Bible Reading Fellowship 1998, £7.99) may be helpful to some laypersons but is of little use to students and preachers.

Useful reprints include *William Kelly* (/Kregel nd, op) and *G. H. Morrison* (2 vols. /AMG 1979, $4.95 each). *Fred Craddock* in the Interpretation series (/Westminster John Knox 1990, £20.00/$29.95) is interesting precisely because he is a fine homiletician. His book is more in the form of expository essays than of commentary. Charles H. Talbert, *Reading Luke: A New Commentary for Preachers* [=British subtitle; American subtitle, *A Literary and Theological Commentary on the Third Gospel*] (2nd ed.; Smyth & Helwys 2003, £15.99/Crossroad 2002, $22.00), focuses on movement of thought but as a result somehow dilutes the connection with the historical Jesus.

Definitely in the "odd" category are two more commentaries, not widely known. Herman Hendrickx, *The Third Gospel for the Third World* is a multi-volume effort, still incomplete. Six volumes have appeared so far; the first covers 1:1–2:52 and others continue at the same pace (/Liturgical 1996–2002, $19.95 each). In short, if this work hopes to make an impact on the so-called Third World, it is being published in a strange place, at a strange price, and with a ponderous pace. T. Josephine Lawler, *Good News for your Autumn Years: Reflections on the Gospel of Luke* (Resource Publications 1994, £9.99/$10.95), is not really a commentary at all but another lovely bit of evidence to the effect that we are becoming more interested in trying to get Scripture to address us in the diversity of our experiences and cultural locations than in listening to what it says. (To recognize that no listener can avoid being culturally located is not the same as self-consciously aiming to control the interpretation by one's cultural location.)

If I were to mention the numerous works that are not commentaries but that nevertheless contribute substantially to understanding the text, this little book would immediately quadruple in size, so in general I refrain. Nevertheless, there are a few works that should be mentioned. Bo Reicke, *The Gospel of Luke* (/John Knox 1964, op), is not strictly a commentary but can be seminal in sermon preparation. I. Howard Marshall's *Luke: Historian and Theologian* (/reprint, Zondervan 1989 [1971], op) was an admirable study in its time but is now very dated. Serious students of Luke-Acts may want to read the collection of essays edited by Leader E. Keck and J. Louis Martyn, *Studies in Luke-Acts* (/Fortress 1980, op), a work that depicted just where the center of contemporary debate on this corpus was a quarter of a century ago. A more popular but more recent book of the same kind is by Mark Allan Powell, *What Are They Saying About Luke?* (Paulist 1989, £7.95/$12.95). Charles H. Talbert, *Literary Patterns, Theological Themes and the Genre of Luke-Acts* (SBLMS 20; /Scholars Press 1974, op) argues that Luke's compositional procedure is akin to steps taken in Suetonius' *Life of Virgil*, Pliny's *Letters*, and Lucian's *How to Write History*, merged with the pastoral model of Paul's letters. It is not clear that Talbert has learned from the severe criticism leveled at his earlier book on the genre of the gospels (especially by David E. Aune), but the fruit of this study resurfaces in Talbert's *Reading Luke*, already listed. Douglas S. McComiskey, *Lukan Theology in the Light of the Gospel's Literary Structure* (Paternoster 2004, np/), evaluates the rather uncontrolled parallels that Talbert offers and develops his own criteria for deciding which ones reflect Luke's actual intentions. One might also mention Robert J. Karris, *Luke: Artist and Theologian: Luke's Passion Account as Literature* (Paulist 1985, op). One very useful volume is Joseph A. Fitzmyer, *Luke the Theologian: Aspects of his Teaching* (Paulist 1989, regrettably op).

3.5 John

The Gospel of John has been as well served by commentaries during the last half-century as any major book in the NT. Inevitably, many treatments are extremely light, and of these lighter contributions only a sampling can be included here. But there is no shortage of major and middling works.

The two-volume work by *Craig Keener* (Hendrickson 2003, £44.99/$79.95 for the set)—a total of 1,636 packed pages—is very impressive. There are few questions Keener has not addressed. Despite the sheer quantity of material, the writing is accessible, so the work can be skimmed until you reach what is of immediate interest to you. It may function in our generation as Brown functioned in the previous generation: the breadth of learning and the bibliographical richness combine to make the work indispensable for the serious student. *R. E. Brown* (AB; 2 vols.; G. Chapman 1971, vol. 1 only, £31.59/Doubleday 1990, $55.00 for vol. 1, $49.95 for vol. 2) is crystal clear and still very useful. At one time it was especially valuable to the student because of its extensive bibliography, but this is now dated. The work's notes and cross references are a mine of information. It is one of the best contributions in the AB series and a fine representative of moderate NT Roman Catholic scholarship. That does not mean that his five stages of literary development, or the sacramentalism he finds running through the text, will command assent among all interpreters. In some ways, Brown's work should be compared with *R. Schnackenburg* (3 vols.; ET Burns &

Oates 1980–82, £100 for the set/Crossroad 1990, $19.95 per vol. pb; the German original has a fourth volume of updating and explanatory essays, 1984), whose allegiance to Roman Catholic tradition is combined with shrewdness, some pastoral concern, and a moderate critical stance. Now severely dated, the ET of the contribution by *Rudolf Bultmann* (/Westminster John Knox 1971, $31.95) is still a provocative classic of continental scholarship but not very helpful to the preacher. Moreover, scholarship has moved on, and both Bultmann's severely precise source criticism and his view of Gnosticism have been so thoroughly shown to be deficient that in retrospect it is hard to see why this commentary exercised the influence in academic circles that it did. *Barnabas Lindars* (NCB 1981, pb op) is a model of concise writing, offering its own solution to the development of the Fourth Gospel in a theory of developing sermon notes; but it cannot compete with the longer works, and it is sometimes pretty dry. *W. Hendriksen* (BoT 1959, £22.95/Baker 1961, op), apart from being dated, may be of some value to the preacher but with the weaknesses inherent in the series already noted in this book. The ET of the posthumously published commentary by *Ernst Haenchen* has appeared in two volumes (Hermeneia; 1984, £28.50 each/$48.00 for vol. 1, $49.00 for vol. 2). This is a major disappointment. Despite the best editorial efforts of Ulrich Busse, Haenchen's student, and of the translator and English editor, Robert W. Funk, the fact remains that the scholarship is terribly dated and thinner and thinner as one progresses through the Gospel. In the latter half, entire pericopae may be summed up in a few lines of comment. Bibliography is slanted, uneven, and dated. The work may be an interesting insight into Haenchen's mind and scholarship in the closing years of his life, but it is a shame to allot the space in so prestigious a series to a half-finished and obsolete contribution. This volume, we are told, is slated to be replaced in due course.

Among the major works on John, one of the best one-volume treatments of the Greek text is still that of *C. K. Barrett*, in the revised edition (SPCK 1988, £45.00/Westminster, op). Although Barrett stands needlessly free from John's historical claims, especially in the passion narrative (compare, for instance, Sherwin-White on the trial), this work is nevertheless not only elegantly and lucidly written, but also usually profound in its grasp of John's theological message and rightly skeptical about many modern literary and historical reconstructions. *Andreas J. Köstenberger* (/BECNT; 2004, $44.99) is a conservative commentary replete with many references to earlier works, which means it picks up on one of the strengths of the commentary by *Leon Morris* (/NIC; rev. ed.; 1995, $50.00), whose work is an encyclopedic treatment from the strictly "earthly-historical" view of Jesus' ministry. This is one of the major conservative commentaries on John, and its footnotes are a mine of quotable material. Sometimes the style is choppy, and some theological and historical questions are not probed very deeply. The predecessor to Morris's work in the NIC series, by *Merrill C. Tenney* (op), has not been superseded by Tenney's further contribution to EBC (vol. 9 bound with Acts as a separate paperback, £9.99/$15.99). Unfortunately this latter treatment is so thin, dated, and sometimes even naive that it can safely be given a miss. Two fairly recent commentaries that lay claim to the evangelical tradition are by *George R. Beasley-Murray* (WBC; 1987, rev. ed. 1999 [Thomas Nelson], £189.99/$39.99) and *D. A. Carson* (Pillar; 1991, £28.99/$44.00). The former is rather thin for the first two-thirds of the Gospel and then becomes very rich indeed, especially in the passion narrative. Some readers will be less than convinced by the source-critical "solution" to the challenges of chapter 20. The revised edition of 1999 primarily signals a change in publisher from Word to Thomas Nelson. A quick comparison of the two editions disclosed no change in substance in the actual commentary, though the new introduction interacts with more recent literature. Carson's work is rather more difficult for me to assess.

Recent commentaries that, so far as length is concerned, are in the middle range, include the following. *Gerald L. Borchert* has written the two volumes for the NAC series (on John 1–11 [1996, $29.99] and John 12–21 [2002, $29.99]). This commentary is easy to follow but tends to be bland. When there are two or three opinions about some matter, Borchert often finds reasons to support all of them. *Thomas L. Brodie* (2nd ed.; OUP 1997, £22.95 pb/$35.00 pb) reads John from a literary perspective and offers many suggestive insights, but the work is too narrowly focused to be one's primary commentary on this Gospel. *J. Ramsey*

Michaels (NIBC; 1995, £8.99/$15.95) writes crisply and in a nuanced fashion but leaves more questions open than he needs to. The SP entry on the Gospel of John, written by *Francis J. Moloney* (Liturgical 1998, $39.95), is well written but not distinctive. It tends to be sharp when it comes to following the narrative flow, while ducking some of the toughest historical questions. In my view, it is a fair bit more sacramentarian than the Evangelist is. *Herman Ridderbos*'s 1987 commentary written in Dutch has now appeared in English (Eerdmans 1997, £24.99/$44.00). This is a major contribution, primarily because it is theologically much richer than most commentaries. Ridderbos interacts with major theological themes from across the history of the church. Although he is obviously conversant with critical issues, and on some points expresses his opinions (often in notes or excursuses), his focus is on theological reflection called forth by John's Gospel. *Ben Witherington III* has written a learned but thoroughly accessible commentary on John. Its title betrays its focus: *John's Wisdom: A Commentary on the Fourth Gospel* (Westminster John Knox 1995, £27.50 pb/$44.95 pb). Witherington always writes well, but I remain unpersuaded that Wisdom is an important, still less a controlling, theme in John, not even in his Christology. *D. Moody Smith Jr.* (ANTC; 1999, /$28.00) brings to his commentary a lifetime of the study of this Gospel, so despite its accessibility it is packed with nuanced judgments offered from a perspective that is moderately critical of the book's historical claims but that still seeks to be edifying.

Other recent or fairly recent commentaries on the Gospel of John include: *Rodney Whitacre* (IVPNTC; 1999, £11.99/$24.00)—one of the stronger volumes in the series: I am not sure why it has not achieved more prominence; *Colin Kruse* (TNTC; 2003, £11.99/$16.00), whose work on John is certainly competent, but whose volume will probably not attract the attention it would have thirty years ago, as there is now much more "competition"; Peter F. Ellis, *The Genius of John: A Composition-Critical Commentary on the Fourth Gospel* (Liturgical 1986/1984, op); *G. S. Sloyan* in the Interpretation series (/Westminster John Knox 1987, £17.99/$29.95); and *Kenneth Grayston* (Epworth 1990, £7.50/[in the U.S. ed., belonging to a new "Narrative Commentaries" series] TPI 1990, $14.95). None of these latter three—Ellis, Sloyan, Grayston—is substantial enough to compete with the major commentaries. Ellis and Grayston sometimes provide insight into the movement of thought in the text. All three are overly skeptical about John's witness to history. The "social science" commentary on John by *Bruce J. Malina and Richard L. Rohrbaugh* (Fortress 1998, $20.00) offers insight into the dynamics of conflict, both in Jesus' day in Palestine and between the church and the synagogue at the end of the first century. Most of the best of this material is found in the bigger commentaries, and without the social-science jargon. I always feel a bit ambivalent about this genre of commentary. The emphasis on the social relationships, all at the horizontal level, provides a salutary anchoring in the historical context of the first century—surely a highly commendable goal. Nevertheless, sometimes the social-science categories are anachronistic. Worse, the effect of reading *only* this sort of commentary is to miss the *theological* dimension that both John and Jesus judged to be of the first importance. *Stanley B. Marrow* (Paulist 1995, £17.99/$19.95) has provided a "reading" of the Gospel of John rather than a commentary (this is Marrow's distinction). In fact it is a section-by-section commentary pitched at the lay level and written from a mainstream Catholic perspective. The contribution of *Barclay M. Newman* to the Translator's Handbook series (/UBS 1993, $37.99) is one of the ablest in the series (though the constraints of the series must be kept in mind). The NIVAC on John is by *Gary M. Burge* (2000, /$29.99).

Specialist interest books that read as if they are uncertain about whether or not they are commentaries include two that aim to help those who are preaching or teaching John's Gospel: Lamar Williamson, *Preaching the Gospel of John* (/Westminster John Knox 2004, $24.95), and Dick Lucas and William Philip, *Teaching John: Unlocking the Gospel of John for the Expositor* (Christian Focus 2002, £5.99/$8.99). Comparing the two is a salutary experience. Another not-quite commentary is the contribution of *Mark Edwards* in the new Blackwell series (BBC; 2003, £70.00 hb or £19.99 pb/2004, $74.95 hb or $31.95 pb), whose purpose is to provide the "reception history" of the biblical books it treats (see §1.2.3, above).

The BNTC/HNTC contribution by *J. N. Sanders and B. A. Mastin*, originally published in 1968, is again out of print. *John Marsh* (Pelican;

1971/1968, op) offers comments that are sometimes suggestive and fresh but frequently uneven. The replacement volume for this series, by *Andrew T. Lincoln*, has been announced, but I have not yet seen it. *R. V. G. Tasker* (TNTC; 1960; reprint, 1983, £9.99/op) is brief and to the point but now so severely dated as not to be on anyone's list of priorities.

J. H. Bernard (ICC; 1923, 2 vols., £45.00 each/$89.95 each) writes with all the individuality, if not eccentricity, that some might expect from an Irish archbishop. The work is thoroughly uneven, occasionally good, but the best of his material has inevitably been culled. Among other reprints of older works are *E. W. Hengstenberg* (2 vols.; /Kregel nd, $36.95 each); *Alfred Plummer* (again op); and *David Thomas* (2 vols. in 1; /Kregel [1885] 1980, op). *William H. van Doren* (orig. 1872, again op) is in some ways a strange work. Its endless stream of "one-liners" can be suggestive to preachers who have done their exegesis before picking up this book. In a class by itself is the critical translation, by Fabian R. Larcher, of *Thomas Aquinas* (/Magi 1980, $35.00). This commentary varies from the good to the masterful. It is always worth consulting, even if on critical issues it is of course hopelessly dated. The thoughtful reader will always discern practical applications if he or she ponders the remarks of *F. Godet* (2 vols. in 1; /Kregel [1885] 1980, op). Both of *B. F. Westcott*'s two commentaries, one on the Greek text and the other on the English, are now regrettably op. If they are disappointing this is because they have been thoroughly picked over by later scholars. Westcott offers thorough exegesis with hints at applications that are there for the discerning reader, but the reputation of the commentaries grew when there was little better. Moreover, his exegesis was done when scholars were more tightly tied to classical Greek than to Hellenistic Greek. His works are worth consulting but no longer the first priority.

Marcus Dods wrote the commentaries both in the EGT series (the entire five-volume set, ed. W. Robertson Nicoll, is unfortunately op) and in the EB series (2 vols.; op). Dods is old and semi-liberal but often suggestive and practical. *G. H. MacGregor* (Moffatt; 1928, op) is disappointingly colorless. *Alan Richardson* (TBC; 1964, op) is not at his best on John and fails to live up to the standard he achieves in other writings. *A. M. Hunter*'s small commentary (CBC; 1965, £17.99/op) is much more useful. *J. C. Fenton* (NClar; 1979, op) and *W. E. Hull* (Broadman 9, bound with M. D. Tolbert on Luke, 1970, /$24.99) are both too brief to be of great help. *D. Moody Smith Jr.* has written the ProcC contribution (1986, /$15.00), a 128-page collection of nine essays that constitute less of a commentary (though John 1, 9, and 16 receive closer attention) than a penetrating summary presentation of the state of Johannine scholarship when Smith wrote. The commentary by *Mark W. Stibbe* (SAP 1993, £25.00/$54.95) in the "Readings" series is short (224 pp.) and priced too high. It attempts a narrative-critical and reader-response reading of John, self-consciously ignoring historical considerations. Stibbe does not think that the entire Gospel is fiction, but in the end retreats to the rather tired assumption (which, strangely, he repeatedly calls "my proposal") that this is "charismatic history"—i.e., it is historical tradition interpreted creatively by the aid of the Spirit. What this means in terms of genuine extra-textual referentiality he never tells us, however, because his entire focus is narrative-critical. It is the sort of claim with which everyone from the most naturalistically inclined liberal to the fundamentalist might cautiously agree, and therefore it means little. What narrative critics might do well to recall is that no biblical writer thinks that men and women are saved by mere ideas—no matter how interesting, intricate, and charismatic those ideas—but by those real entities to which the ideas refer.

By far the best of the "popular" commentaries is that of *F. F. Bruce* (reprint, Eerdmans 1996, $11.99 pb/1994, $22.00 pb). This provides a straightforward exposition in 424 pp. of the text as it stands with virtually no consideration of critical problems (though the alert reader will often detect the sagacity that has gone into critical decisions before pen touched paper). Written at about the same level is the very useful volume by *Robert Kysar* (ACNT; 1991, £10.99/1986, $17.25). A few other popular works may be mentioned, but most of these are not worth a great deal of time: *George W. Macrae* (/Doubleday 1978, op); *Lesslie Newbigin* (1982, op); *Robert E. Obach and Albert Kirk* (Paulist 1979/1981, op). Two slim volumes by Robert Kysar, *John the Maverick Gospel* (Westminster John Knox 1986, £9.99/Presbyterian Publishing Company 1993, $17.25) and *John's Story of Jesus* (reprint [orig. 1984],

Wipf & Stock 2003, $14.00), add little to his more important ACNT volume. The book by *Fred B. Craddock* (KPG; 1986, op) has its interest because of Craddock's skill as a homiletician. The work by *Thomas E. Crane* (/Alba 1980, $5.95 pb) is less a commentary on the Fourth Gospel than a popular exposition of John, 1 John, and Revelation emphasizing how John interprets his own experience of knowing God. The book is steeped in Roman Catholic tradition. The same is true of *John Wijngaards* (MBS; 1991, £11.99pb/1986, $16.95 hb or $12.95 pb), who adopts a critical stance akin to Brown or Schnackenburg, frequently finds "mysticism" in the text, and is much interested in the community behind the text. Raymond Brown, *The Gospel and Epistles of John: A Concise Commentary* [and thus not to be confused with his AB volumes] (Liturgical 1988, £6.99/$9.95), is so brief (136 pp.) it can be given a miss. In addition to his NCB commentary, *Barnabas Lindars* has also produced the NTG volume on John (1990, £10.95/Cornell University Press, $25.95). The slim volume by Donald Guthrie, *Exploring God's Word: A Guide to John's Gospel* (1986, op), is very thin indeed, but the inductive approach might help some laypersons in their personal Bible study if they can get hold of a copy. *John G. Mitchell* (1982, op) is wordy, based on the KJV (it does not even raise the text-critical questions at 5:3 and 7:59–8:11), and not particularly reliable. The four-volume set of expositions by Leon Morris, *Reflections on the Gospel of John*, has been reprinted in one fat volume (/Hendrickson [1986–90] 2000, $19.97). It will help laypersons and might give some preachers some ideas about how to move from text to people, but should not displace Morris's commentary. Written from the perspective of Catholic devotional literature is the four-volume set by *Adrienne von Speyr*, translated from the German (and written half a century ago). The subtitles of the four volumes are, respectively, *The Word Became Flesh*, *The Discourses of Controversy*, *The Farewell Discourse*, and *The Birth of the Church* (Ignatius 1993, £19.50/$24.95 each). *Richard Burridge* (Bible Reading Fellowship 1998, £7.99/) is very brief, but this little book is strong on following the "melodic line" of the Gospel and no less strong at identifying comparative references within the Gospel, therefore alerting the reader to anticipatory double-meanings and echoes. Charles H. Talbert, *Reading John: A Literary and Theological Commen-*

tary on the Fourth Gospel and the Johannine Epistles (Crossroad 1992, £15.00/Smyth & Helwys, $14.95 pb) is also good at following the story line, but it is too brief to be anyone's first choice, and in any case does not wrestle with historical issues. The two-volume work by *Gordon J. Keddie* (Evangelical Press 2003, $26.99 for vol. 1; 2002, $26.99 for vol. 2), like the contributions of John MacArthur, shows its origins in preaching ministry: it is rather more akin to exposition than exegesis. Sources tend to be older works rather than contemporary ones. It is always worth a rapid skim. The WBComp volume by *Gail R. O'Day and Susan E. Hylen* (2006, $24.95) is quite a strong contribution to a weak series. Other popular commentaries include: *Bruce B. Barton* in the Life Application series (/Tyndale House 1993, $19.99 hb or $16.99 pb), *Philip Wesley Comfort and Wendell C. Hawley* (/Tyndale House 1994, $14.99), *Philip Wesley Comfort* (/Baker 1994, $15.99), *J. Carl Laney* (Moody 1992, £14.25/$21.99), the fine contribution to the BST series by *Bruce Milne* (IVP 1993, £9.99/$20.65), and *Robert W. Yarbrough* (/Moody 1991, $8.99). Brief but not popular, and outrageously priced, is the work by *John J. Kilgallen* (MBC; 1992, £69.95/$79.95).

Before leaving John, perhaps I should mention a few of the myriads of special studies on this Gospel. These keep pouring from the press faster than they can be assimilated, so with only a couple of exceptions I have picked volumes that have been around long enough to have stood the test of time. William Temple's *Readings in St John's Gospel* (Macmillan 1961, op/Morehouse 1985, $8.95) is a minor classic, full of down-to-earth application of (mostly) Johannine themes, although its hermeneutic is sometimes dubious. C. H. Dodd, *The Interpretation of the Fourth Gospel* (CUP 1968, £26.00 pb/$39.95 pb) defends the thesis that the closest parallel to John is the Hellenistic world of the Hermetic writings—a viewpoint few will defend today. Nevertheless, the book remains useful on broader themes and approaches. Leon Morris, *Studies in the Fourth Gospel* (Eerdmans 1969, op), is still useful for some of its thematic studies; its essays on criticism have largely been superseded. But Morris's *Jesus is the Christ: Studies in the Theology of John* (IVP/Eerdmans 1989, regrettably op) includes some really excellent theological essays. Although it does not attempt a systematic exposition of Johannine themes, the second Morris volume is more interesting and stimulating than G. R. Beasley-Murray, *John: Word Biblical Themes* (Word 1989, op); Daniel J. Harrington, *John's Thought and Theology: An Introduction* (Glazier 1991/1990, op); John Ashton, ed. *The Interpretation of John* (IRT; expanded and revised edition 1997, £25.00); or John Fenton, *Finding the Way through John* (rev. ed.; Continuum 1995, £14.99/)—really a slender "running-paragraph" commentary. Two useful surveys, both now rather dated, are those of Stephen Smalley, *John, Evangelist and Interpreter* (2nd ed.; Paternoster 1997, £9.99/$23.00), and Robert Kysar, *The Fourth Evangelist and His Gospel* (/Augsburg 1975, op). Another survey, one that comfortably takes the reader down the middle of the road, is that of R. Alan Culpepper in the IBT series, under the title *The Gospel and Letters of John* (1998, /$20.00). In July 2006 we expect to see Warren Carter, *John: Storyteller, Interpreter, Evangelist* (Hendrickson). Cutting his own thoughtful swath through the secondary literature, D. Moody Smith, *Johannine Christianity: Essays on its Setting, Sources, and Theology* (T&T Clark 1989, $55.00 hb/University of South Carolina Press 1989, $14.95 pb), sets a standard in careful style and reflection even though not all will agree with his conclusions. John Ashton, *Understanding the Fourth Gospel*, has now appeared in paperback (Clarendon 1991, £35.00/$74.00). It is an elegantly written and important volume for the more advanced student. Ashton, a student of Xavier Léon-Dufour, largely focuses on Bultmann, wanting to take what is best from him while avoiding his radicalism, atemporal theology, individualism, and abstraction from historical questions. There are some good treatments of individual themes. The book would have been extraordinarily important if it had been published thirty years ago when the influence of Bultmann was ubiquitous. More accessible is Ashton's much shorter but broadly comprehensive *Studying John: Approaches to the Fourth Gospel* (2nd ed.; Clarendon 1998, £22.99 pb/$55.50 pb). Paul S. Minear, *John: The Martyr's Gospel* (/Pilgrim 1985, op), is analogous to his work on Matthew (see above). R. Alan Culpepper, *Anatomy of the Fourth Gospel: A Study in Literary Design* (Fortress 1987, £11.99 pb/$20.00 pb), was considered ground-breaking when it appeared. It applies the new literary criticism to John and offers many fresh insights. At the same time, his adoption of the nineteenth-century novel as his controlling paradigm leads to not a few anomalies. John W. Pryor, *John: Evangelist of the Covenant People* (IVP 1992, /$23.00), explores covenant-related themes in the Fourth Gospel more thoroughly than anyone else does. The title of John A. Sanford's work discloses its focal point of interest: *Mystical Christianity: A Psychological Commentary on the Gospel of John* (Crossroad 1993 hb, 1994 pb, £17.99 pb/$29.95 pb). No one denies that it is possible to read the text this way, but one may usefully dispute that such a reading succeeds in much more than imposing alien meanings on the text. Marianne Meye Thompson, *The God of the Gospel of John* (/Eerdmans 2001, $22.00), has some very useful material on John's use of "God," knowledge of God, the Spirit of God, and so forth. Andrew T. Lincoln, *Truth on Trial: The Lawsuit Motif in the Fourth Gospel* (/Hendrickson 2000, $29.95), doubtless pushes its theme a bit far—focused studies of this kind almost always do—but it is a fascinating treatment. The little work by Ronald S. Wallace, *The Gospel of John, Chapters 1–11: Pastoral and Theological Studies Including Sermons* (reprint [1992], Rutherford House 2004, £9.99/$17.75), is so odd and eclectic that one wonders why it was published. Finally, my own *The Farewell Discourse and Final Prayer of Jesus* [=U.S. title; British title is *Jesus and His Friends*] is still in print in the UK (reprint, Paternoster 1995, £3.99 pb). It is an exposition of John 14–17.

3.6 Acts

Until a few years ago, the book of Acts was still not particularly well served by commentaries, but this has changed. Pride of place should certainly go to *C. K. Barrett* in the new ICC series (2 vols.; Continuum [1994–98] 2004, £19.99 pb each/T&T Clark 2004, $39.95 each). [NB: As publishers swallow up publishers or, conversely, multiply imprints, it is becoming more difficult for those not in the business to sort out who really is the publisher. In this instance, Continuum has bought out T&T Clark—along with some other publishers, including JSOT Press and Sheffield Academic Press—and for reasons still obscure to me sometimes preserves the T&T Clark imprint and sometimes drops it. It may even use a different imprint on opposite sides of the Atlantic.] The fruit of decades of study, these two volumes offer acute and thought-provoking comments, many of them theological, on almost every page. At the same time, one wonders why, in the face of the evidence, this esteemed author stands as loose to the document's historical claims as he does. There is now also an abbreviated version, prepared by Barrett himself, titled *Acts: A Shorter Commentary* (T&T Clark 2002, £19.99/$39.95). For the busy pastor, this may be the better option. No less important than the larger of these two commentaries, if in briefer compass, is the AB contribution by Joseph A. Fitzmyer (Doubleday 1998, $49.95 pb). Certainly the work of both of these scholars is a breath of fresh air after one has read three other commentaries: *E. Haenchen* (Blackwell/Westminster John Knox, op) is important for the really serious student, but its deviously complex reconstructions of Luke's sources and theological interests, not infrequently in defiance of hard evidence, makes it an unsuitable starting point for most preachers. The critical commentary by *H. Conzelmann* (Hermeneia; 1987, £27.99/$55.00) is tied far too tightly to a modified history-of-religions approach. The source- and redaction-critical interests of Gerd Lüdemann, *Early Christianity According to the Traditions in Acts: A Commentary* (SCM/Fortress 1989, op), are everywhere apparent.

F. F. Bruce has written two commentaries on Acts. The one in the NIC series, lightly revised (£22.99/$44.00), is generally more useful to the preacher, although the one published earlier on the Greek text, and also revised and enlarged before the author's death (Apollos 1991, op/Eerdmans 1990, $39.99), offers substantial technical information. Neither commentary is trite or obvious, but one might have been glad for more theology. Very useful is the TNTC contribution by *I. Howard Marshall* (1983, £9.99/1980 $15.00), who was apparently given more space than the constraints of that series normally allow. This is the replacement for *E. M. Blaiklock* (op) who is amazingly thin on theology, for which coins and inscriptions are no substitute. Quite excellent, though now a bit dated, is the EBC commentary by *Richard N. Longenecker* (bound with John [see above]; available as a separate paperback, Zondervan 1996, £13.99/$22.99)—one of the best in the series. Yet as good as they are, these volumes have now largely been superseded by a selection of more recent contributions. *James D. G. Dunn* (Epworth 1997, £15.95/TPI 1997, $24.00) is not comprehensive enough to belong to the first rank but is worth skimming. *Ben Witherington III* (Eerdmans 1997, $54.00) is very good indeed: his "socio-rhetorical" approach (which in this volume tends to mean no more than that the author is sensitive both to the world of the first century and to the structure of the text) is particularly suited to this sort of biblical book. *John B. Polhill* (NAC; 1992, $29.99) is workmanlike but cannot compete with Witherington; neither can *Beverlay Gaventa* (ANTC; 2003, £16.99/$28.00). The contribution of *Charles H. Talbert* (Crossroad 1997, op/$24.95) is too brief and too narrowly focused on the literary structure to command primary attention. With similar focus, but a little more comprehensive, is the work of *Luke Timothy Johnson* in the SP series (1992, £31.50/$44.95). Very good indeed, considering the limitations of the series, is the commentary by *William J. Larkin* (IVPNTC; £9.99/$24.00). Very helpful for the preacher is the volume by *John R. W. Stott* in the BST series (1994, £11.99/$16.00), whose modeling of the move from exegesis to exposition is *sans pareil*. It is more condensed and focused than the work of similar vision by *James Montgomery Boice* (/Baker 1997, $34.99). Not as good, but worth reading, are *David John Williams* (GNC; metamorphosed into its NIBC form 1993, £11.99/1995, $21.27) and *G. A. Krodel* (ACNT; 1986, £10.99 pb/$17.25 pb). The commentary by *French L. Arrington* (/Hendrickson 1988, $16.95) is not theologically rich but is generally useful if one overlooks the occasionally intrusive semi-Pelagianism. Largely from the stable of liberation theology is the contribution of Justo L. González (/Orbis 2001, $30.00). The commentary by *Jaroslav Pelikan* inaugurates a new series, the BTCB (/Brazos 2005, $29.99), designed to provide a mid-level work rich in theology and suitable for church use—for preaching, teaching, and small groups. This is a helpful antidote to the theologically sterile works sometimes produced by those committed to an old-fashioned historical criticism. Yet the pendulum has swung a bit too far: theology that is too abstracted from the history in which God embedded its disclosure is in danger of being free-floating, rootless.

Johannes Munck (AB; 1967, $29.00 hb) has nothing of the sparkle of his *Paul and the Salvation of Mankind* and is frankly disappointing. *Foakes-Jackson* (1931, op) is abysmal, and it has been suggested that he spent all his inspiration on the monumental classic that he edited with Kirsopp Lake, *The Beginnings of Christianity* (5 vols.; reprinted in the past by Baker but again regrettably op).

The mention of the Foakes-Jackson and Kirsopp Lake classic is doubt-less the place to comment on a new series of similar scope and power. This is the six-volume set, *The Book of Acts in Its First Century Setting*, the vision of Bruce W. Winter, the indefatigable Warden of Tyndale House, Cambridge. The series is published by Eerdmans. Some of the volumes are monographs; others are edited compilations. Most of the volumes contain much more information than even the best-trained preacher needs: the series is designed rather more for scholars than for students and preachers. But if the latter have learned to skim-read, the series will prove invaluable, and the last of the volumes, on the theology of Acts, is indispensable. In the order of the series, the six volumes are: Bruce W. Winter and Andrew D. Clarke, ed., *The Book of Acts in Its Ancient Literary Setting* (1993, op); David W. J. Gill and Conrad Gempf, ed., *The Book of Acts in Its Graeco-Roman Setting* (1994, op); Brian M. Rapske, *Paul in Roman Custody* (1995, $50.00); Richard Bauckham, ed., *The Book of Acts in Its Palestinian Setting* (1995, op); Irina Levinskaya, *The Book of Acts in Its Diaspora Setting* (1996, $50.00); and Bruce W. Winter, ed., *The Book of Acts in Its Theological Setting* (promised for 2006, $38.00). Another volume grew out of this work and deserves very high praise: I. Howard Marshall and David Peterson, ed., *Witness to the Gospel: The Theology of Acts* (1998, /$38.00).

The preacher may still find help in the turn-of-the-century work by *R. B. Rackham* (op). Rackham was a devout high churchman, shrewd in his practical comments. He rightly calls attention to a theology of the church but does so with restraint. The complementary emphasis on witness and mission is stressed by C. F. D. Moule in *Christ's Messengers* (op), which is a study (not a commentary) of the first part of Acts, and very briefly by *R. R. Williams* (TBC; 1965, op). Useful all-round com-mentaries have been produced by *C. S. C. Williams* (BNTC/HNTC;

/Hendrickson [1957] 1987, op) and, more recently, *W. H. Willimon* (Interpretation; Westminster John Knox 1988, £17.99/$24.00), but Barrett, Fitzmyer, Longenecker, Marshall, Witherington, and Larkin are all considerably better. As a practical supplement *J. Alexander's* commentary (reprint, BoT 1992, £16.95/$34.99) suggests various lines of thought. *W. Neil* (NCB; 1982, op) is too brief to give much help where it is most needed. *E. F. Harrison* (/Zondervan 1986, op) was dated before it appeared. Doubtless it would be useful to the general reader. *G. A. Krodel* in the ProcC series (1985, £4.50/1981, $11.00) is too brief to serve as more than a quick supplement, and in any case it has been superseded by his own ACNT volume, already listed. *Lloyd C. Ogilvie* (CC; 1983, $24.99 hb or $18.98 pb) contains useful material but is sometimes more interested in communication than in a careful understanding of the material to be communicated. The lengthy (1,229 pp.) commentary by *Gareth Reese* (College Press 1984, op), written in the tradition of the Restorationist movement, is wordy and not his best work. *Charles H. Talbert* (KPG; 1984, $6.95) is too thin to be of great use.

Numerous other thin expositions flood the market but need take up no space on the preacher's shelf. It may be worth mentioning a handful of them. In the Lutheran tradition stands *Richard Balge* (/Concordia 1995, $10.99); in the believers' church tradition is *Chalmer Ernest Faw* (Herald 1993, op/$24.99). One might also mention *Dennis Gaertner* (/College Press 1995, $19.99) and *R. Kent Hughes* (/Crossway 1996, $24.99). The slim NTG volume by *I. Howard Marshall* (JSOT 1992, £10.95/$14.95) is one of the best in the series but is probably not worth purchasing if one has some of the better volumes already mentioned.

Several distinctive studies should be mentioned. Invaluable for the serious student is W. W. Gasque's *A History of the Interpretation of the Acts of the Apostles*, recently reprinted (/Hendrickson 1985, $14.95 pb). Briefer and a firm critique of the more speculative wing of scholarship on Acts (though now already somewhat dated) is Martin Hengel, *Acts and the History of Earliest Christianity* (SCM 1986, op—though it is available under the title *Earliest Christianity* as a reprint from Xpress Reprints for £8.95). The work by Mikeal C. Parsons and Martin M. Culy, *Acts: A Handbook on the Greek Text* (Baylor University Press 2003,

83

£21.50/$21.50), is not really a commentary but just what its title says. It tends to fall between two stools—between the two or three standard "Linguistic Keys" to the Greek Testament and commentary on the Greek text. Added to the intrinsic limitations of the Feminist Companion series (see §1.2.2, above), the Acts contribution, edited by *Amy-Jill Levine* and *Marianne Blickenstaff*, carries the further disadvantage of an outrageous U.S. price for its 242 pages (T&T Clark 2004, £27.50/$130.00). Well worth skimming is the book by Dennis E. Johnson, *The Message of Acts in the History of Redemption* (/Presbyterian & Reformed 1997, $16.99). One need not agree with every line to see how astutely Johnson reads Acts within a canonical framework. The posthumously published work of Colin J. Hemer, *The Book of Acts in the Setting of Hellenistic History* (originally in the WUNT series, published by Mohr Siebeck; now reprinted by Eisenbrauns 1989, $49.50), is a wonderfully erudite study of the social context of Acts, with countless insights and careful bridling of those uncontrolled theological interpretations that leave the controls of history behind. Read it in a good library. Perhaps the most important literary study of Acts is that of Daniel Marguerat, *The First Christian Historian: Writing the 'Acts of the Apostles'* (CUP [2002] 2004, /$48.00 pb). Not nearly so controlled is Jerome Neyrey, ed., *The Social World of Luke-Acts: Models for Interpretation* (/Hendrickson 1991, $19.95), which sometimes confuses carefully examined social context with comparatively uncontrolled modern social theory. The work by Robert C. Tannehill, *The Narrative Unity of Luke-Acts: A Literary Interpretation*, 2 vols.: *The Acts of the Apostles* (Fortress 1990, £13.99 pb each/$22.00 pb for vol. 1 and $23.00 pb for vol. 2) is the companion volume to Tannehill's study of Luke, already mentioned.

3.7 Romans

Of the writing of commentaries on Romans there is no end. The best Romans commentary now available in English is the work of *Douglas J. Moo* (NIC; 1996, £34.99/$60.00). Its introduction is thin, but Moo exhibits extraordinary good sense in his exegesis. No less importantly, his is the first commentary to cull what is useful from the new perspective on Paul while nevertheless offering telling criticisms of many of its exegetical and theological stances. The combination of the strong exegesis and the rigorous interaction makes the work superior to another recent commentary of similar length, that of *Thomas R. Schreiner* (/BECNT; 1998, $49.99). Only the most poorly trained pastor will prefer Moo's NIVAC commentary on Romans (/2000, $27.99) to his NIC volume. Now slightly dated but still very important is the "new" ICC work by *C. E. B. Cranfield* (2 vols.; 1975–79, £40.00 each/$80.00 for vol. 1, $65.00 for vol. 2). Occasionally Cranfield seems more influenced by Barth than by Paul, but for thoughtful exegesis of the Greek text, with a careful weighing of alternative positions, there is nothing quite like it. An abbreviated (320 pp.) edition is also available that makes fewer demands on the reader (T&T Clark 1985, £19.99 pb/Eerdmans 1985, $35.45 pb).

The two-volume work by *James D. G. Dunn* (WBC; 1988, £21.99 each/$39.99 each) is of course more up-to-date bibliographically and is certainly worthy of diligent study. Nevertheless, one of its controlling foci, viz. the thesis that Paul and his readers are wrestling over the *signs* of membership in the people of God, is rather overdone and is in general too indebted to E. P. Sanders. Another recent and major commentary is the work by *John Ziesler* (TPINT; 1989, £22.99/$40.70), who writes with clarity and frequently takes independent stances that provoke reflection. *E. Käsemann* is available in ET (/Eerdmans [1978] 1994, $40.00). Käsemann is brilliant and infuriating, alternating theologically between the insightful and the tradition-bound (he writes as a deeply committed modern Lutheran). No one who reads him can remain neutral about anything he says. The SP contribution by *Brendan Byrne* (1996, £26.99/$44.95), whose approach is literary-rhetorical and who views the epistle as a call to inclusivism mediated through rhetorical persuasion designed to transform readers through a celebratory presentation of the gospel, is suitably faddish but too often misses Paul's point. Certainly it cannot compare with another Catholic contribution, that of *Joseph A. Fitzmyer* (AB; 1993, op/$50.00), whose exegesis is often magisterial. In many of the crucial passages this work sounds far more Reformed than Catholic. A weakness of the work is that it does not interact seriously with much of the new perspective: Fitzmyer simply ignores it. Some of his short excursuses are worth the price of the volume (e.g., on πίστις Ἰησοῦ Χριστοῦ in 3:21–26).

Other recent commentaries on Romans, all of them at the middle level, include the following. *Peter Stulmacher's* work is now available in English and provides one of the best contemporary "Lutheran" readings of Romans (Westminster John Knox 1994, £22.50 pb/$35.45). *Robert H. Mounce* (/NAC; 1995, $29.99) is sensible and workmanlike but not exciting. Somewhat stronger, yet still useful to laypeople, is the commentary by *James R. Edwards* (NIBC; 1995, £8.67/$14.95). The style of *Kenneth Grayston* (Epworth 1997, £8.95/) is frequently abrasive and the positions too often eccentric. *Jack Cottrell* (2 vols.; College Press 1996–98, /$32.99 each) is one of the better entries in this series. Cottrell is more of a theologian than an exegete, and sometimes that shows. The particular strand of Arminian tradition to which Cottrell belongs is more comfortable with the concept of "original grace" than "original sin." In the Campbellite tradition, water baptism is necessary for salvation. *Luke Timothy Johnson's* "literary and theological" commentary (Crossroad 1997, op/Smyth & Helwys 1999, $21.00) is sometimes helpful in untangling the flow of thought but is too brief for close exegesis—and in any case it is not one of his best efforts. The contribution to the UBS Helps for Translators series, by *Barclay Moon Newman* (1994, /$38.99), is one of the stronger volumes in the series. The treatment of Romans by Stanley K. Stowers, under the title *A Rereading of Romans: Justice, Jews, and Gentiles* (Yale University Press 1994, £38.99 pb/$45.00 hb or $24.00 pb), argues that Romans is not really concerned with categories like sin and salvation, is trying to persuade Gentiles that Christian Judaism will give them the self-mastery they seek, and that this form of Judaism, based on the faithfulness of a Messiah who adapted his approach to meet the needs of Gentiles, offers more hope than a Torah-based form of Judaism. There are so many things wrong with this position that it is hard to know where to begin to criticize it, but at least the book nicely presents one form (but only one) of the so-called new perspective on Paul. *Grant Osborne* (IVPNTC; 2004, £12.99/$23.00) is a competent middle-level introduction to Romans; *Ben Witherington III* (Eerdmans 2004, £21.99/$30.00) suffers a bit, perhaps unfairly, from the fact that it is not up to the standards of some of Witherington's other work (such as his commentary on Acts, above).

It is a cause for great thankfulness that *Adolf Schlatter*'s German commentary has recently been translated into English (/Hendrickson 1995, $29.95). Obviously it is very dated (Schlatter died in 1938), but it is still very good at tracing the line of argument in the epistle. Numerous other helpful commentaries on Romans are available. One of the best for the theological flow of thought in Romans is the work of *Anders Nygren* (Fortress 1949, £8.25 pb/op). Everyone who can do so should grasp his general introductory remarks on pages 16–26. Unfortunately, however, the book is inadequate as a verse-by-verse commentary. Here, apart from those mentioned, one might profitably turn to *F. J. Leenhardt* (1961; regrettably op) or *C. K. Barrett* (BNTC/HNTC; 1957, op pb/$26.95 pb). The latter is good, but not quite as memorable as Barrett's two commentaries on the Corinthian correspondence. Nygren, Leenhardt, and Barrett complement each other admirably. *Karl Barth*'s inspiring earlier commentary (6th ed.; OUP 1969, £11.79/Peter Smith 1991, $35.50 hb or $19.95 pb) is still available. Sometimes Barth comes closer to Kierkegaard than to Paul, but almost anything can be forgiven when Barth shows he has grasped, like Nygren, the heart of this epistle—or rather, like Nygren, that he has been grasped by it. Everyone ought to sample it (e.g., on 3:1ff.). In the same tradition of Lutheran scholarship as Barth, Nygren, and Käsemann, but at a lighter level, is *Roy A. Harrisville* (ACNT; 1980, £10.99/$17.25). Not worth more than a quick skim are *P. J. Achtemeier* (Interpretation; John Knox 1986, £17.99/1985, $29.95) and the two commentaries on Romans by *John Paul Heil*—one published by Loyola Press (/1987, $26.00), and the other, a reader-response commentary, by Paulist (1987, op/$9.95). Brendan Byrne, *Reckoning with Romans: A Contemporary Reading of Paul's Gospel* (Liturgical 1986, op/$23.00), is surprisingly good (see comments on his SP commentary, above). One raises eyebrows here and there, but many old truths are set out in fresh ways. The forty theses at the end of the book are worth pondering. *Leon Morris* (Pillar; 1988, £26.99/$40.00) has produced a workmanlike commentary in traditional mold. Its strength is the seriousness with which it takes the text; its weakness is its failure to grapple with the tenor of Pauline studies since E. P. Sanders (on which more below). *Ernest F. Scott* has been reprinted (/Greenwood [1947] 1979/$25.00 hb).

In the revised edition, *F. F. Bruce* (TNTC; 1986, £9.99/1985, $14.00) repays study, but the work was not as extensively revised as one might have wished. *W. Sanday and A. C. Headlam* (ICC; 1902, £40.00/$79.95) are not as dull as is often supposed. *John Murray* (NIC; [1960] 1996, £19.99 pb/$34.00 pb) will guide you stolidly with the heavy tread of the proverbial village policeman (though with more theology; and note especially the useful appendices and notes); while at the other end of the scale *H. C. G. Moule* (EB; op) will fill your soul with lovely thoughts, even if you have something less tangible at the end than you expected. Oddly enough Moule is better in the CBSC series (/CLC 1899, reprint 1975, $12.99 pb).

C. H. Dodd's commentary (Moffatt; 1932, op) has been described as a classic, although on many passages it is hard to see why. Perhaps it is for no other reason than that he writes well. Sadly, however, he consistently flattens future perspectives into present ones and pushes his own theories at the reader: he is uncomfortable unless he can have a domesticated cross. *T. W. Manson* offers concise but useful comments in the New Peake; *A. M. Hunter* (TBC; 1968, op) sketches some helpful themes. But both are too brief to compete with the heavyweights. *John Knox*'s commentary in IB (vol. 9 binds Acts and Romans; op) has a blind spot about the basis of Pauline ethics. *J. C. O'Neill* (Pelican; op) is so eccentric in his source theories (Paul did not write about one third of Romans) that this is unlikely to be the first commentary to which students and preachers will turn. *M. Black* (NCB; 1989, op) has some strong points but is not a first choice. *E. F. Harrison* (EBC 10, bound with Corinthians and Galatians; now available as a separate paperback, /Zondervan, $15.99) is responsible in his comments but provides little interaction and not much spark. *W. Hendriksen* (/NTC; formerly in two vols., now in one; $39.99) some find helpful; from that tradition, Murray is to be preferred. *Ernest Best* (CBC; 1967, op/$13.95 pb) does not live up to his work elsewhere, doubtless owing in large part to the constraints of the series. Although I have not usually mentioned in these pages the contributions of *The New Interpreter's Bible*, I should here mention the work of *N. T. Wright* (2002; vol. 10 of the series, pp. 393–770), who takes up proportionately more space than some volumes in the series and whose well-written contribution helps demonstrate how he attempts to anchor his brand of the new perspective in the text.

There are many popular-level treatments of Romans, most of which will not be noticed here, and a few choice reprints. *F. L. Godet* (Kregel 1982, op/$26.99 hb or $21.99 pb) is not at his best on Romans but still worth skimming. *Charles Hodge* (reprint, BoT 1989, £14.00 pb/Crossway 1994, $19.99 pb) has been eclipsed by Murray, who has been eclipsed by Moo. In some ways the reprint of *Robert Haldane* (/Kregel nd, $30.99 pb) is more important. *Hermann Olshausen* (/Kregel nd, op) sometimes offers independent interpretations that are worth pondering. *John R. W. Stott* in the BST series (1994, £11.99/$16.00) is fine exposition but not as telling, I think, as his treatment of Acts. *D. Martyn Lloyd-Jones*'s ten-volume exposition (nine volumes, not published in sequential order, but covering 1:1–8:39, are available from BoT/Zondervan 1970–1989, prices ranging per vol. from £15.00–£18.00/op; the tenth vol., on Rom. 9, seems to be available only from BoT 1991, £13.95/) is probably not the model most preachers should imitate, but the set is easy to read, and Lloyd-Jones sometimes offers material one is hard pressed to find elsewhere—in addition to the wealth of his practical application of Scripture. Read it if you are a fast reader. In shorter compass is James Philip, *The Power of God: An Exposition of Paul's Letter to the Romans* (N. Gray 1987, op). Other expositions, considerably briefer than Lloyd-Jones, include *James Montgomery Boice*'s four volumes (/Baker [1991–1995] 2005, $24.99 pb each) and the one-volume exposition by *R. Kent Hughes* (/Crossway 1991, $21.99). The two volumes by *John MacArthur* (Moody 1991–1994, £14.99 each/$26.99 for vol. 1, $25.99 for vol. 2) are sometimes closer to exposition than to commentary. Of the brief commentaries, I shall mention only three. *David Lyon Bartlett*'s brief contribution (WBComp; 1995, $19.95) focuses on several of Paul's grand themes (viz. the oneness of God, God's righteousness, Paul's use of the Hebrew Scriptures, and the emergence of the new age in Jesus Christ) and manages to read the entire epistle in these terms. *Bruce B.*

Barton contributes the volume to the LABC (/Tyndale 1992, $14.99). *R. C. Sproul* (FoB; 1999, £14.99/) in short compass develops the themes of Romans along traditionally Reformed lines.

Only rarely have I in this volume mentioned brief study guides, but I cannot hold back from mentioning *R. Bower* (SPCK 1975, op). Designed for students in the so-called Third World, this little book is straightforward, attractively so, and its illustrations, many of which are drawn from the Third World, are refreshingly novel to the Western reader. At the other end of the spectrum, a major work from the patristic period has for the first time become available in English. Origen's commentary on Romans has long been lost, of course, but Rufinus translated it into Latin, and this early Latin translation has now been rendered into English by Thomas P. Scheck, *Commentary on the Epistle to the Romans by Origen, from the Latin Translation of Rufinus* (Catholic University Press, two vols., 2001–2002, £30.95 each/$39.95 each). Scheck kindly sent me his manuscript as he worked on the translation, so I had the privilege of reading this work through before it was sent to press. The translation is superb. The work itself is not what most pastors need for preparation for next Sunday's sermon: the distance between contemporary hermeneutics and the hermeneutics of Origen's world is very substantial. But for advanced students, this pair of volumes is a treasure trove, bringing to light the exegesis of one strand of the patristic period, and returning to view the theological struggles faced by our forebears in the faith.

Recently there has been a spate of books introducing Paul, his background, his theology, and his letters. One of the best of the recent ones is the work by Rainer Riesner, *Paul's Early Period: Chronology, Mission Strategy, Theology* (Eerdmans 1998, /$50.00). Of the brief volumes, one of the best is that of Joseph A. Fitzmyer, *Paul and His Theology: A Brief Sketch* (/Prentice-Hall 1989, $27.80 pb). Neal Flanagan, *Friend Paul: His Letters, Theology and Humanity* (Glazier 1991, op/1986, $9.95), is very elementary but generally competent. Most of these books do not treat all the Paulines, judging some of them to be deutero-canonical; Flanagan omits the Pastorals, and dates 1 Thessalonians before Galatians (which is still the majority view). The book by Martin Hengel, in collaboration with Roland Deines, *The Pre-Christian Paul* (SCM 1991, op/TPI 1991, $21.95), is of very great importance, not only for understanding Paul's background and the combination of Judaism and Hellenism from which he springs, but also for the implicit analysis of the theses of E. P. Sanders. The second edition of Leander E. Keck, *Paul and His Letters* (/ProcC; 1994/$15.00), has been superseded by Fitzmyer. Stanley B. Marrow, *Paul: His Letters and His Theology* (Paulist 1986, £9.99/$19.95), can be ignored, as can Marion L. Soards, *The Apostle Paul: An Introduction to His Writings and Teaching* (Paulist 1987, op/$14.95). Harold Weiss, *Paul of Tarsus: His Gospel and Life* (/Andrews University Press 1986, $15.99 pb), is one of the better elementary introductions.

There are countless special studies relating to Romans, only very few of which can be mentioned here. There are stimulating and provocative essays in E. Käsemann, *New Testament Questions for Today* (op), and ibid., *Perspectives on Paul* (reprint, /Sigler 1996, $19.00). G. Bornkamm's *Paul* is still available (Hodder 1975, op/Fortress 1995, $22.00). But the book that has precipitated much of the recent debate on Paul and the law is doubtless that of E. P. Sanders, *Paul and Palestinian Judaism* (SCM 1981, £27.50/Fortress 1977, $30.00 pb). To this must now be added his book *Paul, the Law, and the Jewish People* (SCM 1985, op/Fortress 1983, $23.00 pb). His smaller and more recent *Paul* (OUP 1991, £6.99/2001, $23.00 pb) adds little to his fundamental theses. Many books and essays have either taken Sanders on board or in some measure reacted against him, and inevitably commentaries on Paul are affected as well. The best single-volume assessment of the current state of play on the axis from Sanders to the new perspective on Paul (often referred to as the NPP) is the book by Stephen Westerholm, *Perspectives Old and New on Paul: The "Lutheran" Paul and His Critics* (Eerdmans 2003, $35.00). See also the two-volume work edited by D. A. Carson, Peter T. O'Brien, and Mark A. Seifrid, *Justification and Variegated Nomism*, vol. 1: *The Complexities of Second Temple Judaism*; vol. 2: *The Paradoxes of Paul* (Mohr Siebeck 2001–2004, €54.00 each/ Baker 2001–2004, $89.95 for the set).

Well worth reading if you can pick it up secondhand is W. D. Davies, *Paul and Rabbinic Judaism* (4th ed.; 1980, op). His *Jewish and*

Pauline Studies (1984, also op) is not so cohesive. Nevertheless, these books reflect a lifetime of study and will repay the student or minister who is well enough equipped to handle them. Mention must be made of Seyoon Kim, *The Origin of Paul's Gospel* (reprint, /Coronet 1984, $62.50), who argues that the basic structure of Paul's thought is tied up with his conversion on the Damascus road. In some ways this is an impressive updating of the old work by J. Gresham Machen, *The Origin of Paul's Religion* (op), but in addition to the thesis, the book is studded with valuable discussions and exegeses. His more recent book, *Paul and the New Perspective: Second Thoughts on the Origin of Paul's Gospel* (/Eerdmans 2002, $26.00), extends the defense of his thesis but also interacts tellingly with the new perspective on Paul. Harry Gamble Jr., *The Textual History of the Letter to the Romans* (op), provides an able defense of the unity of the epistle. The dense prose of Martin Hengel and Anna Maria Schwemer in *Paul Between Damascus and Antioch: The Unknown Years* (Westminster John Knox 1997, $17.47 pb) packs in a thorough probing of the background to these "unknown years." The best exegetical and theological discussion of Romans 9 is that of John Piper, *The Justification of God: An Exegetical and Theological Study of Romans 9:1–23*, also regrettably out of print. For those who want a user-friendly introduction to current mainstream thought on Paul, his letters, and their background, in addition to the plethora of New Testament introductions one might consult Charles B. Cousar, *The Letters of Paul*, in the IBT series (1996, £11.99 pb/$20.00 pb). Pitched at the level of the student just beginning the study of Paul is a recent book by John B. Polhill, *Paul and His Letters* (Broadman & Holman 1999, $34.99), a gentle mix of introduction, survey, and theology. Finally, of all the books that wrestle with Pauline theology, in some ways the best is still Herman Ridderbos, *Paul: An Outline of His Theology* (Eerdmans [1975] 1997, $32.00 pb). But that work was written prior to the onset of the new perspective on Paul. Those taken up with that approach certainly include James D. G. Dunn, *The Theology of Paul the Apostle* (/Eerdmans 1998, $50.00). One should certainly not ignore the stimulating compilation of patristic sources achieved by *Gerald Bray* in the ACCS volume (/1998, $40.00).

3.8 1 Corinthians

Before evaluating commentaries that treat 1 Corinthians alone, I should mention four that cover both 1 and 2 Corinthians. *Craig Keener* (NCBC; CUP 2005, £35.00 hb or £12.99 pb/$60.00 hb or $21.99 pb) is written with his customary verve and assurance, but the space limitations (312 pp.) mean that this work is not to be compared with his magisterial commentary on John (see above). Not all will be persuaded by all of his arguments on some of the most contentious interpretive issues, of course, but he is always a thoughtful dialogue partner. *Ben Witherington III* has produced another "socio-rhetorical" commentary, one that covers both epistles (Paternoster 1995, £24.99/Eerdmans, $38.00). Like all his work, it is accessible and talks good sense. I remain unpersuaded that his treatment of wisdom is quite right and that all his reconstructions are the best possible inferences of the text. *Gerald Bray* has produced the ACCS volume (/1999, $40.00), which gives ready access to many patristic treatments of these epistles. The beginning of competition for the ACCS series is found in the rich work of *Judith L. Kovacs* (ChB; Eerdmans 2005, £19.99/$35.00). It has a feel of being less "bitty," less atomistic, than the ACCS volume. Kovacs covers only 1 Corinthians, not both Corinthian epistles. Though his work is now slightly dated, *F. F. Bruce* on both the Corinthian epistles (NCB; 1981/1980, op) is astonishingly good for the space allotted: the work is a marvel of condensed learning and especially wise on certain contentious issues (e.g., the χαρίσματα), but the brevity of the discussion forces the reader to turn to longer works. One can still pick it up secondhand but usually at an outrageous cost.

The best commentary on the Greek text of 1 Corinthians is *Anthony C. Thiselton* (NIGTC; 2000, /$80.00). The work is very impressive. Over 1,400 pages long, it could easily have been a ponderous volume of massive learning and impenetrable prose. But Thiselton has outdone himself. Every section I scanned was well written, accessible (for readers of this sort of series!), and penetrating. It provides not only detailed exegesis but also a tracing of the main issues of interpretation from the Church Fathers to the present. The work will doubtless prove too difficult for poorly trained pastors, but for those with the requisite skills this commentary will prove an invaluable resource.

The best general commentary on this epistle is a toss-up: it is either *Gordon D. Fee* (NIC; 1994, £29.99/$54.00) or *David Garland* (/BECNT; 2003, $49.99). Despite one or two extraordinary lapses (e.g., his treatment of 1 Cor. 14:33b–35 as an interpolation), Fee's commentary is lucid, informed, sensible, and written with great verve. Occasionally the passion that marks this commentary is grating—especially when Fee is passionate about a position with which one disagrees! Garland's work is no less competent and interacts with another ten years of work. Scarcely less important are *Raymond F. Collins* in the SP series (1999, £39.95 pb/$39.95 pb), and *C. K. Barrett* (BNTC/HNTC; 2nd ed.; Black 1971, op/Hendrickson [1968] 1993, $29.95). In both cases there is a wealth of useful material, and those with no Greek can follow the argument. Collins is more descriptive and less theological than Barrett. *Roy A. Harrisville* (ACNT; 1987, op/$26.00) and *Marion L. Soards* (/NIBC; 1999, $14.95) are both useful but cannot compete with Fee and Thiselton. Charles H. Talbert, *Reading Corinthians: A New Commentary for Preachers* [=British subtitle; American subtitle is *A Literary and Theological Commentary on 1 and 2 Corinthians*] (SPCK 1987, £15.00 pb/Crossroad, $16.95), is often helpful in identifying literary patterns and flow but is theologically rather thin and rarely treats the text verse by verse. He thinks 2 Corinthians 10–13 was written before 2 Corinthians 1–9.

In the past, the standard critical commentary on the Greek text of 1 Corinthians was that of *Hans Conzelmann* (Hermeneia; 1975, £27.99/$48.00). His extensive bibliography and full citation of parallel texts, not to mention his frequently penetrating discussion, make him useful to students who can handle Greek. Moreover, most of the cited texts provide full ET. But the substantial weaknesses of the work cannot be ignored (cf. the review in *Themelios* 1 [1976]: 56–57)—and in any case it has been thoroughly outstripped by Thiselton (above). The old ICC volume by *Archibald Robertson and Alfred Plummer* (2nd ed.; 1914, £50.00/$100.00) adduces many parallels without the benefit of translation, but this work is one of the better ones in the series. Another work largely on the Greek text is *J. Héring* (ET from 2nd French ed.; 1948, op), which maintains an unconvincing partition theory but is full of useful and sprightly comment. The little book by *R. St. John Parry* (CGT; 2nd ed.; 1937, op) is helpful to the student trying to sharpen Greek skills, if it can be obtained secondhand. Recent middle-level commentaries on 1 Corinthians include the following: *Craig Blomberg* in the NIVAC series (1995, £19.99/$24.99) is perhaps the best of them, with *Richard B. Hays* (/Interpretation; 1997, $24.95) following closely behind, and *Graydon F. Snyder* (Mercer University Press 1992, £17.95/$18.95) following more distantly. *Richard A. Horsley* (ANTC; 1998, £12.99/$21.00) highlights the socio-political context of 1 Corinthians and the clash between the religious viewpoints of Paul and of the Corinthian believers.

Other commentaries deserving honorable mention include *J. S. Ruef* (Pelican; 1977, op), which is competent and makes good use of space but does not add much to Barrett and Bruce; and *Leon Morris* in the revised edition (TNTC; IVP 1986, £9.99/Eerdmans 1988, $14.00), who provides useful remarks on some Greek words behind the ET. *James Moffatt* (Moffatt; 1938, op) is still worth scanning on the religious, social, and historical background in Hellenism. *C. T. Craig* (IB 10, bound with 2 Corinthians and Ephesians; 1953, op) adds some useful comments here and there, but not more. *W. F. Orr and J. A. Walther* (/AB; 1976, $32.50) provide a lengthy introduction that is concerned with Paul's itinerary and its relation to Acts, frequently for the (laudable) purpose of rehabilitating Acts; but it contains too little information on Corinth, and the comments themselves vary from the very detailed to the very thin. Karl Barth's *The Resurrection of the Dead* (reprint of 1933 ed., /Ayer 1977, op) is still an outstanding work. Although this is primarily an exposition of chapter 15, the first half of the book summarizes the argument of the first fourteen chapters. There can be few better expositions of the grace of God and the frailty of humankind than this little book. It is certainly not a verse-by-verse commentary.

J. B. Lightfoot, *Notes on the Epistles of St. Paul*, has often been reprinted but is out of print at the moment. Lightfoot is always worth consulting, though usually later commentaries have gleaned the best of his work. Available reprints include: *Hermann Olshausen* [on both Corinthian epistles] (/Klock & Klock, $14.75), which varies between the insightful and the eccentric; *Thomas C. Edwards* (/Kregel 1991, $19.99); and *Charles Hodge* (Crossway 1995, £10.99 pb/1996, $17.99 pb), which is not as good as some have thought. Doubtless it was outstanding when there was less exegetical competition, and it is still worth perusing today—but not as a first choice and only if allowance is made for a century of work, including considerable improvement in our grasp of Hellenistic Greek. Bernard O'Kelly has edited *John Colet's* [d. 1519] *Commentary on First Corinthians: A New Edition of the Latin Text, with Translation, Annotations* (Binghamton, NY: Medieval and Renaissance Texts and Studies 1985, $30.00), which will doubtless prove of greater help to students of the Renaissance and of the history of exegesis than to students of 1 Corinthians.

G. *Deluz* (1963, op) is excellent from a practical point of view, when read in conjunction with a commentary like that of Thiselton or Garland. Deluz tends to summarize the best of points from *F. Godet* (2 vols. reprinted as one; Kregel 1982/1977, op). *F. W. Grosheide*, the old NIC work (1953, op) now replaced by Fee, is below par and can be safely skipped. Both *Robert B. Hughes* (Moody 1985, £6.75/$9.99) and *John J. Kilgallen* (Paulist 1987, op/$5.95), though from very different theological backgrounds, share this in common: their books are primarily for the general reader within their respective constituencies. *Kenneth L. Chafin* (/CC; 1985, $24.99 hb or $10.99 pb) can be safely ignored. Alan Redpath's *The Royal Route to Heaven* (reprint, Revell 1993, op/$11.99) is completely unreliable on exegesis, but where his own thoughts happily coincide with the sense of the passage they are remarkably practical. *Marcus Dods* (EB; op) is verbose but worth scanning. *Gordon H. Clark* (2nd ed.; /Trinity Foundation 1989, $10.95) tends to treat the text in a historical vacuum and sometimes reveals more about himself and his beliefs than his ostensible subject, but occasionally there are insightful remarks. *Margaret E. Thrall* (CBC; 1965, £18.99 pb/$25.95 pb) is one of the best of the brief commentaries, but the final essay, on "The Corinthian Letters Today," is rather misleading. *W. Baird* (KPG; 1980, op) and *J. Murphy-O'Connor* (Bible Reading Fellowship 1997, £7.99/Doubleday 1998, $11.95) are both worth scanning. *John MacArthur Jr.* (Moody 1995, £14.99/$26.99) provides more of an exposition than a commentary (see remarks on his work on Matthew). Despite excellent moments, there is too little grasp of the background and such a firm "anti-charismatic" interpretation of chapters 12–14 that the exegesis goes a little awry. Recent popular treatments include *William A. Beardslee* (/Chalice 1994, $7.49 pb), *Peter Naylor* (Evangelical Press 1996, £12.95/), *Richard Oster* (/College Press 1995, $32.99 hb), *Nigel Watson* (Epworth 1992, £7.95/$11.95), and, in the BST series, *David Prior* (1993, £9.99/$15.00). One notch up from the BST volume are the thoughtful contribution of *Alan F. Johnson* (IVPNTC; 2004, £11.99/$22.00) and the contribution of *N. T. Wright* in the Paul for Everyone series (SPCK 2003, £9.99/Westminster John Knox 2003, $14.95).

There are numerous special studies on 1 Corinthians or on the pair of Corinthian epistles, and a few of them deserve mention here. Jerome Murphy-O'Connor, *St. Paul's Corinth: Texts and Archaeology* (/Liturgical 1983, $21.95 pb), is invaluable for those who want more background information. J. C. Hurd Jr., *The Origin of 1 Corinthians* (rev. ed.; 1982, op), provides a detailed reconstruction of the situation at Corinth, but the theory is supported by considerable speculation and highly improbable partition theories. Hurd's work now enjoys less influence than it once did. A quiet little gem is Lewis B. Smedes, *Love within Limits: Realizing Selfless Love in a Selfish World* [=orig. subtitle; recently changed to *A Realist's View of 1 Corinthians*] (/Eerdmans 1978, op), which uses 1 Corinthians 13 as the basis for some thoughtful and sometimes stirring reflections. Ralph P. Martin has written the Word Biblical Themes volume on *1, 2 Corinthians* (Word 1989, op); the same author has published *The Spirit and the Congregation: Studies in 1 Corinthians 12–15* (1984, op). The latter is written in an easy style that belies the work that has gone into it, but I found it more reliable on chapter 15 than on chapters 12–14. D. A. Carson, *Showing the Spirit: A Theological Exposition of 1 Corinthians 12–14* (Paternoster 1987, £4.99/Baker 1987, $20.00), attempts a fairly detailed exegesis of the three chapters specified in the title and a discussion of their relation both to relevant passages in Acts and to modern developments. It includes a full bibliography and detailed notes, though the text itself can be followed by the student without Greek. More popular in level is D. A. Carson, *The Cross and Christian Ministry: Studies in 1 Corinthians* (IVP 1993, £8.99/reprint, Baker 2004, $12.99), a series of expository studies on parts of 1 Corinthians (esp. chaps. 1–4, 9). Wayne Grudem's *The Gift of Prophecy in 1 Corinthians* (/UPA 1982) is now op, but one can still find his argument, if not the focus on 1 Corinthians, in his more recent and general *The Gift of Prophecy in the New Testament and Today* (Kingsway 1988, op/reprint, Wipf & Stock, $27.20). Victor Paul Furnish, *The Theology of the First Letter to the Corinthians* (CUP 1999, £14.95/$22.99) is one of the stronger entries in that series. Probably the two most important recent treatments of the nature of rhetoric and its disputed status in 1 Corinthians are Duane Litfin, *Paul's Theology of Proclamation: 1 Corinthians 1–4 and Graeco-Roman Rhetoric*, SNTSMS 79 (CUP 1994, op), and R. D. Anderson, *Ancient Rhetorical Theory and Paul* (Peeters 1999 [2nd ed.], /$33.00). Bruce W. Winter has produced several works on 1 Corinthians, but perhaps his best is *After Paul Left Corinth: The Influence of Secular Ethics and Social Change* (/Eerdmans 2000, regrettably op). The book is worth trying to find simply to read the careful material on 1 Corinthians 6 regarding homosexuality in the Roman world.

3.9 2 Corinthians

I shall not mention again those commentaries that serve both of the epistles to the Corinthians (discussed above). After years of neglect, the last two decades have attracted a fair bit of attention to 2 Corinthians. It is the most passionate and in some ways the most difficult of Paul's letters.

The best two commentaries on the Greek text of this epistle are those of *Margaret E. Thrall* (ICC; 2 vols.; vol. 1, 1994, £45.00 hb/$100.00 hb; vol. 2, 2001, £50.00 hb/$100.00 hb; 2004/$39.95 pb) and *Murray J. Harris* (NIGTC; 2005, $75.00). Both demand that the reader have a reasonably good reading knowledge of Greek; the one by Harris is more conservative critically than that of Thrall, who embraces a partition theory (she thinks that 2 Corinthians was originally three separate documents). Thrall's treatment of the Greek text is always thorough and thought-provoking but less often convincing. Harris's commentary is just as thorough, more often convincing, and is in any case more pastorally suggestive, and therefore of better value to the preacher.

As for the best single-volume commentaries on the English text, and therefore more widely accessible than the two just mentioned (though of course Greek informs the study), are those of *C. K. Barrett* (BNTC/HNTC; 1973, op/1993, $24.95) and *Frank Matera* (NTLNTM; Westminster John Knox 2003, £30.00/$39.95). Barrett's is now a little dated, but it is quite outstanding. One may disagree with his breakdown of opponents in chapters 10–13 and with other minor points, but this commentary is one of the "standard" works. That of Matera is in the same class and more recent. Another is the work by *Victor Paul Furnish* (/AB; 1984, $42.50). Much longer than Barrett or Matera, this one leaves few stones unturned and on many points offers sane and thoughtful exegesis. Its wordiness makes it slightly less desirable than the other two. The recent commentary by *David E. Garland* (/NAC; 2000, $29.99) is one of the best in its series. It is less technical than that of Barrett but just as probing in the theological arena. Although I usually do not like the NIVAC contributions very much—too many of their "applications" are slightly forced or trendy—the 2 Corinthians volume by *Scott Hafemann* (2000, £16.99/$27.99) is a superior entry. Of great length and detail is the recent work by *Ralph P. Martin* (WBC; 1985, £19.99/$39.99). As usual, Martin displays a mastery of the secondary literature up to his time of writing, and as usual writes with clarity; but I found the work a little disappointing, too speculative at many junctures and occasionally wrong-headed. *Paul Barnett* (NIC; 1997, £28.99/$50.00) has produced a major commentary that is a joy to read. It is extraordinarily rich on the historical and social circumstances that surround this complicated book. Moreover, it is rich in its biblical-theological reflection (i.e., the author takes pains to tie the theology of this epistle to the theology of the Pauline corpus and sometimes to the entire Bible). But it is somewhat less telling in its interaction with current literature, and it is not always rigorous in its treatment of exegetical fine points. The substantial (470 pp.) commentary by *William Baker* in the CPNIVC (/1999, $32.99)—a product of the Restorationist movement—is one of the stronger contributions to the series so far, but the commentary cannot compete with the contributions of Barrett and Matera, and suffers as well from a disproportionate number of typos. The commentary by *Jan Lambrecht* in the SP series (1999, £23.99/$39.95) is frankly disappointing, not least because at his best Lambrecht is a very competent scholar. For some odd reason the editor of the series allowed him to get away with extreme brevity, no footnotes, and superficial treatment. (The volume on 1 Corinthians in the same series, for instance, is almost three times the length.) The ET of the CNT volume by *Jean Héring* (1965, op) is sprightly and well written but now superseded by more recent works.

Philip Hughes (NIC; 1982, op/$30.00) provides thoughtful and usually reliable comments but lacks verve and power. In some ways it is superseded by *Simon J. Kistemaker* (/NTC; 1997, $39.99), written in the same tradition and one of the stronger volumes in his series. *R. V. G. Tasker* (TNTC; op) is well written and briefly helpful but adds nothing to Hughes. In any case it has been superseded by the new TNTC volume by *Colin Kruse* (1987, £9.99/$14.00)—an excellent addition to the series. Stronger than both of them is the commentary by *Linda L. Belleville* (NIVNTC; 1996, £9.99/$22.00). Though pitched at a middle level, this volume is one of the strongest in its series and should be considered a "must" for serious expositors. *James M. Scott* (/NIBC; 1998, $14.95) is surprisingly full for a relatively brief commentary. Its strength is in its lucid style and its exploration of Jewish background. But too often its most original proposals prove unconvincing, based as they are on fairly speculative connections to some particular "background" stance or other. Scott brushes up so closely to "parallelomania" that readers need to be wary. *A. Plummer* (ICC; 1915, £50.00/$100.00) tends to be pedestrian but is worth picking up secondhand; I cannot imagine paying those prices for a new copy. *F. V. Filson* (IB vol. 10; see above on 1 Corinthians) sometimes adds fresh insight, but not everyone will want to pay the secondhand price for the whole volume. *R. H. Strachan* (Moffatt; 1935, op) obviously had a bad year in 1935. *James Denney* (EB; nd, op) is still very fresh on many issues, but it would seem better if it had not been overrated by some senior evangelicals. *J. H. Bernard* (EGT; five-volume set ed. W. Robertson Nicoll; /Eerdmans 1952, op) is dated but sometimes useful. *M. J. Harris* (EBC vol. 10; see on Romans, above; it is now available as a separate paperback volume, Hodder, op/Zondervan, $15.99) is quite excellent within the strictures of space allotted to it—clearly the best of the four commentaries bound up in this volume. But if you can read Greek, choose his magnificent NIGTC volume (above) instead. *Frederick W. Danker* (ACNT; 1989, op/$17.25) is worth scanning but cannot compete with Barrett and Matera, let alone with Harris and Thrall; the same is true of *E. Best* (Interpretation; 1987, op/$24.95). *Richard P. C. Hanson* (TBC; 1961, op) is slender but worth skimming; much the same can be said for *G. R. Beasley-Murray* (Broadman, op). Barely worth scanning, as far as the preacher is concerned, is the ET of *Rudolf Bultmann* (/Augsburg 1985, op; the German original was 1976, published from class notes of lectures delivered between 1940 and 1952). The contribution to the Paul for Everyone series, written by *N. T. Wright* (SPCK 2003, £8.99/Westminster John Knox 2003, $14.95), is helpfully evocative.

In the BST series, *Paul Barnett*'s work is well done (1988, £8.99/$15.00) but of course is now superseded by his NIC volume (see above). H. D. Betz, *2 Corinthians 8 and 9* (Hermeneia; 1986, £21.95/1985, $38.00) is typical Betz: many parallels, only some of which are exegetically helpful, and too little theological reflection. Despite its title and series, the work by Jerome Murphy-O'Connor, *The Theology of the Second Letter to the Corinthians* (NTT; CUP 1991, £45.00 hb or £16.95 pb/$26.99 pb), is less a theological analysis of 2 Corinthians than a flowing survey with some probing into the social background. *V. George Shillington*'s contribution to the BCBC (/Herald 1997, /$24.99) is considerably stronger than *Geoffrey Grogan*'s contribution to FoB (1996, /$10.99). D. A. Carson, *From Triumphalism to Maturity: An Exposition of 2 Corinthians 10–13* (Paternoster, £1.99/Baker, op—but currently being reprinted), is as the subtitle suggests an exposition of the last four chapters of 2 Corinthians, the most emotionally explosive writing from Paul's pen. For a contemporary series of expositions on the entire epistle, see *R. Kent Hughes* (/Crossway 2006, $24.99).

Of monographs on this epistle there is now no shortage, but perhaps the most important one for the preacher is Timothy B. Savage, *Power Through Weakness: Paul's Understanding of Christian Ministry in 2 Corinthians* (SNTSMS 86; CUP 1996, £60.00 hb or £21.99 pb/$85.00 hb or $37.99 pb).

The record of greater or lesser disappointments includes *Francis T. Fallon* (NTM; 1980, £1.00/$12.95); Alan Redpath, *Blessings out of Buffetings: Studies in Second Corinthians* (/Revell 1965, $11.99)—see the comments on his volume on 1 Corinthians; and the following five reprints: *Roy L. Laurin* (/Kregel 1985, $11.99); *H. C. G. Moule* (/CLC 1976, $8.99); *Charles R. Erdman* (orig. 1929, often reprinted, op again); *David J. Valleskey* (/Concordia 1995, $14.99); *Nigel Watson* (Epworth 1993, £7.95/$13.00); and the NTG volume by *Larry J. Kreitzer* (1996, £12.99/$25.95).

3.10 Galatians

There have been several major commentaries on the Greek text written within the last three decades, each in its own way outstanding. *Hans Dieter Betz* (Hermeneia; 1980, £27.99/1979, $58.00) provides voluminous parallels from the Greco-Roman world, including almost endless comment on the kinds and style of argument Paul deploys. Betz's use of Jewish background is disappointingly thin, and the salvation-historical structure of parts of Paul's argument is sometimes overlooked. Ostensible parallels cannot substitute for accurate exegesis. I do not think he has got to the bottom of Paul's understanding of the relationships between law and grace. The best critique of Betz's approach is that of Philip H. Kern, *Rhetoric and Galatians: Assessing an Approach to Paul's Epistle to the Galatians* (SNTSMS 101; CUP 1998, £55.00/$75.00). *F. F. Bruce* (NIGTC; 1982, £29.99 hb or £14.99 pb/$40.00 hb) evenhandedly weighs virtually all of the relevant literature up to the time of writing and presents the flow of the argument with a deft touch and readable prose. Occasionally the reader will want more theological punch—for example, on the law/grace, old covenant/new covenant fronts, and in more detailed dialogue with E. P. Sanders and his followers. Criticisms aside, these two commentaries are very important if the student or preacher can work with the Greek text. Not surprisingly, homiletical hints are few and far between, and neither interacts tellingly with the new perspective on Paul (which is scarcely surprising granted when they were published). We need a commentary on the Greek text that accomplishes more than these two do.

Based on the Greek text, but more accessible to the reader without much skill in Greek, are the commentaries by *Richard N. Longenecker* (WBC; 1990, £1.99/$39.99) and *Ronald Y. K. Fung* (NIC; 1994, £21.99/$32.00). The latter is workmanlike and a substantial improvement over its predecessor in the series; the former is especially strong on the Jewish roots of the debate but perhaps weaker on Spirit-passages. The commentary by *J. Louis Martyn* in the AB series (/1998, $42.50 hb or $39.95 pb) is a major tome (614 pp.) rich in the idiosyncratic interpretations that mark most of Martyn's work. But it requires a fair bit of knowledge to spot the serious breaches and misinterpretations that abound in it. In short, the specialist will benefit from the shrewd insight that characterizes many of Martyn's comments without being easily snookered by the unfounded idiosyncrasies, but others will find it more difficult to separate wheat and tares (and in this case, we do not want to offer the advice, "Let both grow until the end."). *Frank J. Matera* (SP; 1992, £26.99/$34.95) writes with admirable clarity, but he is more indebted to one form of the new perspective on Paul than the text warrants. There is not much to choose from between Matera and *James D. G. Dunn* (BNTC/HNTC; 1993, £19.99/$29.95). The NIVAC volume by *Scot McKnight* (/1995, £19.99/$22.99) is clear and accessible, but it, too, reduces too many of the "law" issues to questions of boundary markers and social identity. *Ben Witherington III* (Eerdmans 1998, £19.99/$35.50) is typically well written and sometimes casts an eye on useful application. Witherington's interest in rhetorical structure will not convince readers at every point, but it does reinforce the sense of coherence in the argument of the epistle. The translation of *Dieter Lührmann's* German commentary into English (Fortress 1992, £14.99/$24.75) is almost inexplicable: it is thin (160 pp.), interacts with almost no one, and adopts, with little discussion, a more-or-less traditional Lutheran reading without really arguing the case.

The commentary by *Timothy George* (/NAC; 1994, /$29.99) is *sui generis*: it is far richer than most substantial commentaries on Galatians in its survey of earlier treatments, not only from the Reformation period but also much earlier as well. Correspondingly, however, it is a bit thin in its interaction with major positions today. That makes this an ideal commentary to be read in conjunction with three or four others that have opposite propensities. While we are reflecting on the *sui generis*, this is probably the place to mention four other works: *Paul Nadim Tarazi* (St. Vladimir's Seminary Press 1994, £11.99/$18.95) provides a commentary in the Orthodox tradition; *Mark J. Edwards* provides us with access to a host of patristic materials in his ACCS volume on Galatians, Ephesians, and Philippians (/1999, $40.00); *Philip F. Esler* (Routledge 1998, £62.50 hb or £19.99 pb/$120.00 hb or $36.95 pb) provides not so much a commentary as a highly creative wrestling with the text, not only embracing the new perspective, but also maintaining a rigorous deployment of rhetorical criticism and social-scientific method. The result is a hermeneutical proposal that he calls "interculturalism": the reader keeps going back and forth between his or her own culture and the culture of the text, being molded by the experience. Along the way, Esler, who must reject much of the historicity of Acts, ends up taking positions remarkably similar to those of the old Tübingen school. And finally, *Eric Plumer* has edited *Augustine's Commentary on Galatians* (OUP 2003, £56.00 hb or £18.99 pb/$110.00 hb or $35.00 pb).

John Bligh (St. Paul 1969, op) has produced a 500-page commentary that represents the best of modern Roman Catholic scholarship in England, although he still includes oddly-loaded comments on such issues as the role of Peter. The structuralism is plentiful, perhaps forced at times. Although there is much to admire, I am not convinced that Paul always speaks for himself. The commentary by *Donald Guthrie* (NCB; 1982/1981, op), as we have come to expect from this author, is always clear, ordered, and on the whole valuable, even if sometimes not very incisive. The developments bound up with the new perspective on Paul since Guthrie wrote inevitably make the work sound dated. The CBC commentary by *William Neil* (1967/1966, op/$18.95 pb) is stimulating but too brief to demand much attention. The contribution by *Charles Cousar* (Interpretation; 1986, £14.99/1982, $24.95) is even less full, but is one of the better contributions to this series. The ET of the work by *Ragnar Bring* (1961, op) is oriented toward Lutheran dogmatics.

E. de W. Burton (ICC; 1921, £40.00/op) remains a monument to thoroughness and concern over detail. The additional notes are often useful, as are the comments, but the latter have largely been superseded by Betz and Bruce. Concise and occasionally useful to the preacher are the practical commentaries by *K. Grayston* (1957, op) and *G. S. Duncan* (Moffatt; 1934, op). The latter can often be picked up secondhand. *H. N. Ridderbos* (NL/NIC; 1953, op) has now been superseded by its replacement volume by *Ronald Y. K. Fung* (see above). *William Hendriksen* (NTC; Galatians in one volume: BoT 1969, £5.50; Galatians and Ephesians bound together: BoT 1981, £21.50/Baker 1979, $24.99) is warm-hearted but too frequently misses the historical and theological nuances of the text. *R. Alan Cole* (TNTC; 1983, £9.99/1989, $14.00) is sometimes helpful in bringing out the meaning of Greek terms simply and concisely. *James Montgomery Boice* (EBC 10; see on Romans; now available in pb, Hodder, op/Zondervan [with Ephesians], $15.99 pb) is helpful enough for the preacher but adds nothing to, say, Guthrie. The commentary by *Sam K. Williams* (ACNT; 1997, £11.99/$20.00) concisely evaluates an array of options and ably if briefly defends the views of its author, including the occasional idiosyncratic interpretation (e.g., his well-known interpretation of πίστις Χριστοῦ).

J. B. Lightfoot (reprinted as a four-volume set on Galatians, Philippians, Colossians, and Philemon, including the fourth volume on *Notes on the Epistles of St. Paul* [i.e., unfinished work on other Pauline epistles]; /Hendrickson 1981, $79.95) has been mined so thoroughly by others that he hardly ever adds anything to more modern treatments. *Martin Luther*'s work is available in at least two English-language editions. The first is somewhat abridged (Clarke 1953, £12.50/reprint, Kregel 1987, $18.99); the second is vols. 26–27 of the Concordia set of *Luther's Works*, ed. J. Pelikan (1962–63, $30.00 each). He writes with power and passion, but his work is simply too verbose for most twentieth-century readers, who in any case need to make allowance for Luther's concern with the Pope in places where Paul is concerned with Moses. J. Skilton has edited *Machen's Notes on Galatians* (unfortunately op). This is not strictly a commentary, nor does it cover the entire epistle, and in any case it is rather dated. But the student who works through it carefully will learn what exegesis is all about, how to do it, and even how to apply it to a contemporary setting (although some of the historical allusions reflect the struggles of a past generation). In some ways it anticipates the recent book by Moisés Silva, *Interpreting Galatians: Explorations in Exegetical Method* (/Baker 2002, $24.00)—an updated and enlarged edition of *Explorations in Exegetical Method: Galatians as a Test Case* (/Baker 1996, $22.99), no less stimulating and certainly far more current. Specialists may appreciate the ET of Desiderius Erasmus, *Paraphrases on Romans and Galatians*, ed. Robert D. Sider, tr. John B. Payne et al. (vol. 42 of the Collected Works; University of Toronto 1984, £72.00/$53.00). They will also appreciate the availability of the classic commentary by *William A. Perkins* (/Pilgrim [1617] 1990, $19.95 pb), one of the strategic transitional figures in the move from the continental to the English Reformation. I should add that John Calvin's forty-three *Sermons on Galatians* have been freshly and admirably translated (BoT 1997, $46.99).

A number of smaller, lighter commentaries have appeared, including one by *Edgar Krentz* [on Gal.; John Koenig on Phil. and Philemon; Donald H. Juel on 1 Thessalonians—all bound together] (ACNT; 1985, £10.99/$17.25), and another by *Leroy E. Lawson* (/Standard 1987, $12.99 pb). The latter is not up to snuff, and the former are too brief to compete with more substantial work. *John MacArthur Jr.* (/Moody 1987, £14.99/$22.99) often makes some very good pastoral points that are helpful to the preacher, but he should not be used on his own (see comments above on his Matthew commentary). The same could be said for the devotional classic by Lehman Strauss, *Galatians and Ephesians* (/Loizeaux 1980, $14.99). The best of the lighter commentaries is doubtless that of *Walter G. Hansen* (IVPNTC; 1994, £9.99/$20.00). Less penetrating is *L. Ann Jervis* (/NIBC; 1999, /$14.95), who holds that union with Christ is more of a central theme in Galatians than justification. Somewhat more traditional is *Leon Morris* (IVP 1996, £9.99/$15.99).

Many popular expositions have been written on Galatians, but only a few of them deserve skimming, let alone thoughtful reading. One of the best is John Stott's *Only One Way: The Message of Galatians* (BST; 1992, £9.99/1988, $15.00). William Barclay's little study *Flesh and Spirit* (St Andrew 1978, op) is helpful. *W. A. Criswell* (1980) is now out of print, but in this case the loss is not great. The Baker reprint of *Charles Erdman* is now itself out of print. The contribution of *Carlyn Osiek* (NTM; 1981, £1.00/$6.95 pb) is one of the thinnest in the series. One can safely give a miss to *Kenneth L. Boles*, who covers both Galatians and Ephesians in one volume in the CPNIVC series (/1993, $32.99). *Edgar H. Andrews* (Evangelical Press 1996, £10.95/) is worth skimming; with less urgency, so are both *Bruce B. Barton* in the LABC (/1994, $14.99) and *John B. Fenton* (Bible Reading Fellowship 1996, £7.99/). The volume by *Philip Graham Ryken* is solid Reformed exposition (/Presbyterian & Reformed 2005, $24.95). The contribution of *Stanley Saunders* on *Philippians and Galatians* (/Geneva Press 2001, $9.95) is not more than an elementary Bible study.

The work by Gerhard Ebeling, *The Truth of the Gospel* (Fortress 1985, op), is a cross between a running exposition and an essay in systematic theology. Based on the Greek text (which is then both transliterated and translated), the book is fresh and stimulating, but like so many other tomes written from a Lutheran and existential perspective, it is frequently right in what it affirms and wrong in what it denies—especially on crucial topics such as faith, truth, law, and works of the law. The study by John Barclay, *Obeying the Truth: A Study of Paul's Ethics in Galatians* (T&T Clark 1988; reprint Regent College 2005, $34.95) is very strong when it focuses on the exegesis of the last two chapters and worth the most careful reading for that reason. But I am not sure that Barclay, who has bought into rather more of E. P. Sanders than seems justifiable, has rightly sorted out how Paul thinks of the relationship between law and grace. Somewhat irritating is Barclay's tendency on occasion to be so kind to Paul's opponents that he makes Paul sound like a twit.

Monographs on Galatians continue to pour from the presses. Perhaps I should mention two more, precisely because they are written from distinctive perspectives: John Buckel, *Free to Love: Paul's Defense of Christian Liberty in Galatians*, Louvain Theological and Pastoral Monographs 15 (Peeters 1993, £25.00/Eerdmans 1993, $25.00), and Bruce W. Longenecker, *The Triumph of Abraham's God: The Transformation of Identity in Galatians* (Abingdon 1998, £19.99/$25.00). I should mention one extraordinarily influential monograph with whose thesis I disagree: Richard B. Hays, *The Faith of Jesus Christ* (2nd ed.; /Eerdmans 2001, $25.00).

3.11 Ephesians

The best English-language commentary on Ephesians is now that of *Peter T. O'Brien* (Pillar; 1999, /$40.00). He has thoughtfully absorbed and filtered the best material from earlier commentaries, but has made his own contribution by sticking close to the text, tracing out the theological argument with care and precision. He is able to deploy the various "tools" in the arsenal of New Testament exegetes without giving too much weight to any of them; he is able to reflect on historical and social circumstances without swallowing up the theology implicit in much social science. For sheer volume, of course, the prize must go to *Harold W. Hoehner* (/Baker 2002, $59.99). Although it is unsurpassed on many fronts (e.g., his treatment of many of the issues of "introduction"), O'Brien's contribution is the better general-use commentary. More technical, but not stronger theologically, is the new ICC contribution by *Ernest Best* (1998, £55.00/$110.00), who on many passages is superb but tends to set the author of Ephesians (whom he judges not to be Paul) over against Paul, treating some of the arguments in the epistle as falling below Paul's standards. Strangely, he thinks that the principalities and powers, though hostile, are capable of being redeemed. The "household code" is "pastorally unrealistic" and "defective" even within a first-century setting. Best has also written the slim guide in the NTG series (1993, £9.99/$25.95). *Andrew T. Lincoln's* commentary (WBC; 1990, £19.99/$39.99) is excellent on many points. But on grounds that strike me as entirely unconvincing (and that O'Brien takes on), Lincoln argues that Paul himself did not write Ephesians, and occasionally this stance affects his exegesis (e.g., on 4:7ff.). On the whole, however, it does not, and the commentary on most passages is superb, both at the level of dealing faithfully with the text and at the level of theological reflection. Lincoln's grasp of the eschatology of the epistle is profound. Not as thorough, but nevertheless an impressive work, is the ET of *Rudolf Schnackenburg* (2nd ed.; T&T Clark 2002, £25.00 pb/$49.95 pb).

The lengthy commentary of *Markus Barth* (/AB 2 vols.; 1975, $40.00 for vol. 1, $34.00 for vol. 2) is painstakingly detailed, but even so, the theology sometimes dictates the exegesis. More advanced students can scarcely afford to be without it. But Barth's treatment of certain themes crucial to the epistle sounds more like his father than like Paul. In some ways, a more useful commentary is that of *C. L. Mitton* (NCB; 1982, op/1981, $17.00). This is a good and accessible work, even if Mitton continues to support his earlier defense of non-Pauline authorship. He apparently had no opportunity to interact with A. van Roon's substantial defense of the traditional position in *The Authenticity of Ephesians* (NovTSup 39; Brill 1974, £77.75/$133.50). (Intriguingly, Lincoln reviewed van Roon at one point and offered additional reasons to support van Roon's position. Thus his commentary marks a change from his earlier published stance.) The metamorphosis from GNC (1984) to NIBC is accomplished successfully in *Arthur G. Patzia's* work on Ephesians, Colossians, and Philemon (1991, £7.99/$14.95). The result is a competent but unexciting middle-level commentary, easily accessible. The NIVAC is by *Klyne Snodgrass* (1996, £18.99/$26.99). The SP contribution by *Margaret Y. MacDonald* (/2000, $44.95) covers both Ephesians and Colossians. (Her title, rather gratingly, is *Colossians and Ephesians*, reflecting her estimation of their order of composition. But whoever thought canonical order reflected compositional order?) The strength of her work is her close comparison of the two epistles: by examining the subtle differences, she puts their different perspectives into sharp relief and ties these to the reconstructions she develops with the aid of social science approaches. But although the work is very competently done, too often the differences are exaggerated, and the reconstruction of the social identities of the readers is more fragile than she thinks. *Francis Beare* (IB 10; details above) is scarcely worth scanning. *Ernest Scott* (Moffatt; 1939, op) is erratic and uneven. *Francis Foulkes* (TNTC; 1989, £9.99/$14.00) offers good value for its size. The ACNT contribution to Ephesians and Colossians, by *Walter F. Taylor Jr.* and *John H. P. Reumann*, respectively (1985, op/\$17.25), is adequate but undistinguished. A separate ACNT volume by *Pheme Perkins* (1997, £11.99/\$20.00) is not up to the standard one expects from her. The volume by *Thomas R. Yoder Neufeld* (/BCBC; 2002, \$29.99) is a solid but not an exceptional treatment of Ephesians. The commentary by *Adrienne von Speyr* (Ignatius 1996, £9.95/\$12.95), translated from the German, is frankly traditionalist (opponents label her "patriarchalist") on the relevant passages. It is fairly brief and is essentially Catholic devotional literature.

H. K. Moulton (with Colossians; Epworth 1962, op) has a good eye for practical lessons but should not be used on its own. *E. K. Simpson*, in an earlier edition of NL/NIC (1957/1958, op), provides some helpful comments on individual words, but on the whole the work is an erudite disappointment. His vocabulary is impressive, but not much else is. The replacement by *F. F. Bruce* (on Ephesians, Colossians, and Philemon; 1995, £22.99/1994, \$40.00) marked a notable advance; his work is well worth reading even though Lincoln has on most points now eclipsed him, and O'Brien has eclipsed both of them. One should also not overlook Bruce's more popular exposition (Pickering and Inglis 1978, op); it can still be picked up secondhand. Neither *J. A. Allan* (TBC; 1959, op) nor *G. H. P. Thompson* (CBC, with Colossians and Philemon; 1967, op/\$22.95) is very significant. *A. Skevington Wood* (in EBC 11; op; bound separately, \$15.95 pb) is not worth much time. The recent volume by *Walter L. Liefeld* (IVPNTC; 1997, £9.99/\$20.00) packs a lifetime of thoughtful study of this epistle into fairly small space.

Brief commentaries on the so-called "prison epistles" (Ephesians, Philippians, Colossians, and Philemon) bound in one volume have been written by *J. Leslie Houlden* (Pelican; 1977, op) and *George B. Caird* (NClar; 1976, op). They pack a great deal into small scope, especially the latter. By contrast, the work on Ephesians, Philippians, and Colossians by *George Johnston* (CB; 1967, op) is disappointingly thin just where one needs the most guidance. The Interpretation commentary on Ephesians, Colossians, and Philemon by *Ralph P. Martin* (1992, £14.99/\$24.95) is too slender to be worth much time. The book by

John F. MacArthur Jr. (/Moody 1995, £14.25/$25.99) shares the same strengths and weaknesses as his treatment of Matthew. I have already mentioned the ACCS volume (above, on Galatians).

The old-fashioned standby on the Greek text is *J. Armitage Robinson*, now regrettably op. It can still be useful, though its best points have been culled by later writers. *B. F. Westcott* (op) is almost as good, and his additional notes repay rapid perusal. *S. D. Salmond* (EGT; the entire set, /Eerdmans 1952, op) completes this older classical trio. *Charles Hodge* (reprint, BoT 1991, £9.95/$21.99 hb or $17.00 pb) is even older but solid and often theologically very suggestive. One should certainly not overlook *John Calvin's Sermons on Ephesians* (reprint, BoT 1974, £17.95/1979, $35.99), which can still be marvelously suggestive to preachers. The classic work by *George Stoeckhardt* has now been translated (/Concordia 1987, $19.95).

Of the more popular treatments, the studies by *H. C. G. Moule* (/Kregel [1937] 1977, op) still offer good value for the money when they can be picked up secondhand. The eight volumes of sermons by *D. Martyn Lloyd-Jones* (BoT 1976–1985, various prices from £8.50 to £17.95—some of them hb only, some available in pb/Baker 1983, $90.00 pb for the set) are eminently worth reading but only if you read very quickly. Worth reading, too, is John R. W. Stott, *God's New Society* (BST; 1984, £9.99/1988, $16.00). *Lionel Swain* (NTM; 1981, £1.00/op) is not worth the time, though the price is right. The expositions by *James M. Boice* (/Zondervan 1988, op) and *R. Kent Hughes* (/Crossway 1990, $21.99) are models of their kind, demonstrating the shape of faithful expository ministry, and thereby serving as models for preachers. *Homer Kent Jr.* (Moody 1971, £6.75/$9.99) is not as good. The little book by Donald Guthrie, *Exploring God's Word: Bible Guide to Ephesians, Philippians and Colossians* (Hodder & Stoughton 1984, op/Eerdmans 1985, op), is designed to encourage inductive Bible study among laypeople. Other popular commentaries include *Bruce B. Barton* in the Life Application series (/1996, $14.99); *Leon Morris* (/Baker 1994, $17.99); *Steve Motyer* (Crossway 1994, £4.99/Baker 1996, $10.99); *Stuart Olyott* (Evangelical Press 1994, £6.95/); and *R. C. Sproul* (FoB; 1994, £6.99/). Popular treatments in a less conservative tradition include *Larry J. Kreitzer*

111

(Epworth 1997, op); *Martin Kitchen*, in the New Testament Readings series (Routledge 1994, £52.50 hb or £17.99 pb/$105.00 hb or $33.95 pb)—an outrageous price for a 168-page book of this nature; and *Bonnie Bowman Thurston*, covering, astonishingly, Colossians, Ephesians, and 2 Thessalonians (Crossroad 1995, op/Smyth & Helwys 1999, $19.00 pb).

For those who read French, the commentary by *Charles Masson* (CNT; op) is outstanding, though well culled by Lincoln. Specialists may also want to read Edgar J. Goodspeed, *The Meaning of Ephesians* (/University of Chicago Press 1933, op). Once again, patristic experts are making the fruit of their study available: Ronald Heine has given us *The Commentaries of Origen and Jerome on St. Paul's Epistle to the Ephesians* (OUP 2002, £56.00/$125.00).

3.12 Philippians

The best commentary on the Greek text of Philippians is the magisterial work by *Peter T. O'Brien* (NIGTC; 1991, £39.99/$50.00). O'Brien has read and thought through everything of importance up to his date, with the result that he gives *reasons* for his exegetical decisions. At the same time, this commentary is theologically rich, even if its prose is sometimes pedestrian. The treatment of the so-called "Christ hymn" (2:5–11) is superb. Virtually as good (though with slightly different strengths), and more accessible, is the NIC volume by *Gordon D. Fee* (/1995, $42.00). Fee could not be boring if he tried. The zest of his prose makes him exciting to read, and his scholarship is always rigorous. Occasionally the dogmatism of his style, which makes him so enjoyable to read because his passion for the truth is contagious, makes him slightly irritating to read because he is casually dismissive of points of view not so easily written off. Equally accessible to students and pastors who have not kept up their Greek is *Gerald Hawthorne* (2nd ed.; WBC; 2004, $39.99). Hawthorne's strength is the culling of scholarship up to his time. But his work presents some highly implausible comments (e.g., on 1:27–30, where his reading of the Greek is just about impossible, and on the "hymn," where he opts for the Byzantine reading to solve the parallelism). The second edition of *Moisés Silva* (/BECNT; 2005, $29.99) is a good deal stronger than the first, in that it interacts more acceptably with other positions. The commentary is excellent when its relative brevity is taken into account and is especially strong in tracing the flow of the argument. The recent BNTC/HNTC commentary by *Markus Bockmuehl* (1997, £19.99/1998, $29.95) is very good. Bockmuehl has read everything relevant and is as comfortable in the Greco-Roman background as in the Jewish background. He is as able to wrestle with theological issues as with historical matters. His treatment of the "form" of God in the so-called "Christ hymn" is especially suggestive and is taken up by *Stephen E. Fowl*, whose contribution marks the debut of a new series (/THNTC; 2005, $20.00) that promises a fresh "theological reading" in the hope of bridging the gap between exegesis and systematic theology. This will be a series to watch. Nevertheless, I think it is probably over-promising. Fowl's best theological points are found in the larger commentaries, which also include a lot of material that he skips over. The NIVAC is by *Frank Thielman* (1995, £13.99/$22.99); it is not flashy, but it is one of the more substantive entries to this series. The NAC contribution by *Richard B. Melick* (/1991, $29.99) is workmanlike but not outstanding. The ACNT volume on Philippians and Philemon by *Carolyn Osiek* (2000, £12.99/$21.00) is very keen to relate Philippians to current discussions of slavery and women's issues. The commentaries on Philippians and Philemon by *Bonnie B. Thurston* and *Judith M. Ryan* (SP; 2005, £28.99/$39.95) are competent enough but not ground breaking or particularly penetrating. Too slim to belong to the first rank, but still worth reading, is the volume by *I. Howard Marshall* (Epworth 1992, £7.95/). Farther down the list of fairly recent commentaries is *Fred B. Craddock* (Interpretation; 1986, £17.99/1984, $24.95). The shorter commentary of *Gordon D. Fee* (IVP 1999, op) can be safely skipped if one has his NIC volume.

Among the list of slightly esoteric volumes on Philippians, the ACCS contribution (providing access to patristic sources) should not be forgotten (see above on Galatians). For translators, *I-Jin Loh* has produced the UBS Handbook on this epistle (/1995, $26.99), while *J. Harold Greenlee* has written the "exegetical summary" published by SIL (1992, op). The volume by Ben Witherington III, *Friendship and Finances in Philippi* (TPI 1994, £14.99/$24.95), is too brief to belong to the first rank, and the series to which it belongs, New Testament in Context, announces to the reader where the focus is. The volume by *Jeffrey T. Reed* (SAP 1997, op/$120.00) is a highly technical and highly competent discourse analysis of the epistle. If you want more on that approach, don't buy the book unless you are as rich as Croesus: that's what libraries are for.

J. B. Lightfoot continues to be reprinted, not only bound with other volumes (see on Galatians), but also in a separate commentary on this Epistle (/Crossway, £9.99/$15.99), and his additional essays are still valuable. *M. R. Vincent* (ICC, including Philemon; 1897, £30.00/$59.95) adds virtually nothing to the more recent commentaries. *F. W. Beare* has just come back into print (NCB; [1959] 1988, £10.99 pb/$16.00), but the work is too brief and defends a partition theory that sometimes affects the exegesis. His comments are sometimes very astute (e.g., on righteousness). *Ralph P. Martin* has written two commentaries on this epistle, one of them now extensively revised. The earlier one, in the TNTC series, was originally published in 1960 and was reprinted in a paperback edition in 1983. Given its scope, it is excellent and still worth obtaining secondhand (it is op). In the most recent edition of this TNTC commentary, however (1987, £9.99/1988, $14.00), Martin revised his work to bring it into line with his NCB commentary on Philippians (1981/1980, op). It is packed with useful interaction with the secondary literature, but by this point Martin was influenced by Käsemann's "odyssey of Christ" approach to the Philippians hymn and related material. I find this interpretation exegetically weak. The matter is well discussed by O'Brien. *J. H. Michael* (Moffatt; op) contains many useful hints for the preacher, if the commentary is read in conjunction with a more rigorous work. *F. F. Bruce*, after the usual metamorphosis from GNC, has contributed the NIBC volume on Philippians (1989, £7.99/$21.27). It is brief and to the point. A solid, verbose, and unexciting treatment can be found in *W. Hendriksen* (bound with Colossians and Philemon; BoT 1988, $17.95/Baker 1979, op).

The two commentaries on the prison epistles I mentioned in the Ephesians section, by *J. L. Houlden* and *George B. Caird*, are worth scanning. A number of older or shorter commentaries are generally unremarkable. *F. Synge* (TBC; 1951, op) is too brief to give much help (except for a good comment on Christ as "Adam in reverse" in 2:1–11). The substantial work by *Jean-François Collange* is still available in English (Epworth 1979, op/1979, $12.95) and even in translation is forceful and provocative, but his judgments can be questioned too often to make this a first choice. *K. Grayston* (with 1 and 2 Thessalonians; /CBC; 1967, $9.95 pb), in spite of its brevity, is sometimes worth scanning. *H. A. A. Kennedy* (EGT; 5 vols.; Eerdmans 1952, op) and *Jacobus J. Müller* (NIC; [1955] 1985, op) are severely dated and were never that outstanding in the first place. The same must be said for *Alfred Plummer* (op). *Homer A. Kent* (EBC; now available in paperback bound with Colossians and Philemon; Zondervan, £9.99/$15.99) is brief and was dated when it was written; it sometimes has useful remarks on individual words. *H. C. G. Moule* is still worth purchasing secondhand (/Kregel 1977, op), largely because of the warm, devotional tone that bathes his exegesis.

Specialists will be glad that Ralph P. Martin's *Carmen Christi* is again in print (/IVP 1997, $30.00 pb). For bibliographical thoroughness up to its time of publication, it is impossible to beat. I remain unpersuaded that Martin's exegesis of Phil. 2:5–11 is right: see, among others, O'Brien.

Countless popular studies on Philippians have been prepared, many with the word "joy" in the title somewhere. The best of them include: A. T. Robertson, *Paul's Joy in Christ*, reprinted by Baker (1979) but again out of print; J. Alec Motyer, *The Message of Philippians: Jesus our Joy* (BST; 1984, £9.99/1988, $15.00); James M. Boice, *Philippians: An Expositional Commentary* (/Zondervan 1982, £13.95/$19.99); John Gwyn-Thomas, *Rejoice . . . Always!* (BoT 1990, £5.00/), a study in Philippians 4; Earl Palmer, *Integrity in a World of Pretense: Insights from the Book of Philippians* (/IVP 1991, op); David Ewart, *A Testament of Joy: Studies in Philippians* (/Kindred Productions 1995, op); Gordon Samuel, *Joy: Philippians* (Ambassador Productions 1995, £4.50/); and *Gerald F. Hawthorne*, who in addition to his WBC commentary has produced the Word Biblical Themes volume (1987, op). Other popular works on Philippians include D. A. Carson, *Basics for Believers: An Exposition of Philippians* (reprint, IVP 2004, £2.99/Baker 1996, $9.99); Ian Coffey,

Philippians: Free To Be the People of God (Crossway, op/Baker 1994, $7.99); John Phillips, *Exploring Philippians* (reprint, /Kregel 2002, $23.99); and several volumes that treat more than one of the epistles: *Anthony Lee Ash* on Philippians, Colossians, and Philemon (College Press 1994, $29.99), *Bruce B. Barton* in the Life Application series on the same books (/1995, $14.99), and *Daniel J. Harrington*, again on the same books, in the Spiritual Commentaries series, the equivalent of what Protestants would call devotional commentaries (New City 1997, £7.50/$9.95).

3.13 Colossians/Philemon

I will not discuss again in this section commentaries on Colossians that are bound with commentaries on Ephesians, most of them popular, one or two of them important (see entries on Ephesians under MacDonald, Thurston, Martin, and Patzia); or commentaries on Colossians bound with commentaries on Philippians (see previous section, entries under Osiek, Ash, Barton, and Harrington).

Several major commentaries on Colossians press for attention. Probably the best is still that of *Peter T. O'Brien* (WBC; 1987, £19.99/1982, $39.99). Based on an exact exegesis of the Greek text, it is nevertheless presented with sufficient clarity to satisfy most readers who do not know the language. It is a mine of useful bibliography and helpful interaction with secondary literature (up to its time of writing), and wends its way through voluminous material without losing its theological moorings. I hope the author will update the work. A little more up-to-date is the NIGNT volume by *James D. G. Dunn* (/1996, $45.00)—very useful but not as theologically nuanced as O'Brien. The AB volume by *Markus Barth and Helmut Blanke* (1994, op/$39.95), though longer than the previous two, is not up to their standard. With respect to the work of *E. Lohse* (Hermeneia; 1971, £24.99/$43.00), the reader should not be put off by its rejection of Paul's authorship, for it too contains a wealth of clear and useful comment. A little more Greek is required of the reader, though parallels are usually provided both in the original and in translation. The 1987 German commentary by *Petr Pokorný* has been translated into English (/Hendrickson 1991, $24.95), but it adds little to the other two. Despite the relative dates, Pokorný does not seem to know of O'Brien. Pokorný comments only on Colossians; the other two include Philemon.

On the whole, I have been reticent about the NIVAC, but do not avoid the volume on Colossians by *David E. Garland* (/1998, $27.99). Another recent commentary is the replacement TNTC volume by *N. T. Wright* (1987, £9.99/1988, $14.00). In some ways this work is superb, and it is written with verve and style. I am not entirely persuaded by Wright's reconstruction of the situation Paul is confronting. The BCBC volume by *Ernest D. Martin* (1993, £13.95/$24.99) is one of the stronger ones in the series. The contribution to the ANTC series by *David M. Hay* (2000, £12.99/$22.00) is not exegetically detailed, but it devotes considerable space to the role this epistle has played in the development of Christian thought and to its bearing on some contemporary issues. The IVPNTC entry by *Robert W. Wall* (1993, £9.99/$22.99) cannot compete with volumes already mentioned, nor is it one of the stronger volumes in its series—though it is nicely written.

In a class by itself is the inaugural EGGNT volume by *Murray J. Harris* (with Philemon; Eerdmans 1991, op/$30.00). This is not quite a commentary, yet it is more than a commentary. Harris intends to help students and pastors read through the Greek text intelligently, making appropriate exegetical decisions at every point. He has gleaned the best of the grammars and commentaries with this purpose in mind and thus saves the student a lot of time. Nevertheless, his work does not replace the best commentaries, which offer far more theological reflection *based on* the text (but without always showing how it is *tied to* the text). Those who want shortcuts will give Harris a miss; those who want to improve their own exegetical skills on the way toward biblical theology will find him a very helpful guide. His book presupposes that the reader has had at least a couple of years of Greek. In some ways the work feels dated, as Harris has no patience with (knowledge of?) linguistic developments, including aspect theory. Access to patristic comments can be found in *Peter Gorday* (/ACCS; 2000, $40.00), bound with 1–2 Thessalonians, Philemon, and the Pastoral Epistles.

The EKK volume on Colossians by *Eduard Schweizer* has been translated into English but is no longer available (/Augsburg 1982, op). His
work combines full knowledge of the relevant literature with some down-
to-earth exegesis. I have often encouraged exegesis students to work
through *C. F. D. Moule* (CGT; 1957, £13.99 pb/$49.95 hb or $21.99
pb), a slim book that helpfully encourages the student to work with the
Greek text. *F. F. Bruce* is useful as usual in his NIC volume on Ephesians
(replacing Simpson), Colossians, and Philemon (1984, £22.99/$42.00).
At about the same level is *Ralph P. Martin* (NCB; 1982/1981, op), in
some ways a better work than his corresponding volume on Philippians.
Less detailed and technical, and with some direct aids for the preacher,
is his work *Colossians: The Church's Lord and the Christian's Liberty*
(reprint, /Wipf & Stock 2000, $21.00).

The EKK volume on Philemon is separate from the EKK volume on
Colossians (see above), and there is no ET, but the German original by
Peter Stuhlmacher is generally excellent (1975). Somewhat slimmer on
Philemon is the volume by Allen Dwight Callahan, *Embassy of Onesi-
mus: The Letter of Paul to Philemon* (/TPI 1997, $17.95). *Markus Barth
and Helmut Blanke*, who wrote the AB commentary on Colossians (see
above), have also written the ECC series volume on Philemon (2000,
£22.95/$40.00). It is very large (539 pp.) and includes a substantial
examination of slavery in Paul's day as background for the exegesis. It
is slightly ponderous in style. But perhaps the best general-use commentary on Philemon is the commentary by *Joseph A. Fitzmyer* (/AB
2000, $21.95).

The reprint of *J. B. Lightfoot*, already mentioned (see on Galatians),
makes available his usual thorough but now dated treatment of the Greek
text, to which the ICC by *T. K. Abbott* (1897, £50.00/$100.00) adds
surprisingly little. *G. Johnston* (1967, op) is disappointing, as is *E. F.
Scott* (see on Ephesians). *F. W. Beare* (IB 11; op) still repays study. *H. K.
Moulton*'s helpful little work was noticed in the Ephesians section. In
addition to *William Barclay*'s DSB on Philippians, Colossians, and the
Thessalonian epistles (St Andrew/Westminster 1975, £6.50/$29.95 hb
or $12.95 pb), one of the best in the DSB series, there is his useful book
entitled *The All-Sufficient Christ* (St Andrew 1978, /$6.95). *Herbert*

Carson wrote the old TNTC volume (1960, op), but it was one of the weaker entries in the series and has now been eclipsed by its successor (by N. T. Wright; see above).

Specialists will be interested in the collection of essays on Colossians edited by Fred O. Francis and Wayne A. Meeks, *Conflict at Colossae* (/Scholars Press 1973, op). The study by Norman R. Petersen, *Rediscovering Paul: Philemon and the Sociology of Paul's Narrative World* (Fortress 1985, op), is a mixed bag. Its vocabulary is drawn from the world of sociology, which is sometimes deployed in too heavy-handed a fashion. On many points Petersen is creative and suggestive, but he does not appear to know enough about first-century social history (as opposed to sociology) to warrant his conclusions. The recent book by Brian J. Walsh and Sylvia C. Keesmaat, *Colossians Remixed: Subverting the Empire* (Paternoster 2004, £11.99/IVP 2004, $22.00) is really a species of exposition: it moves from commentary to application in a seamless way. If you share the authors' view that globalization and current American foreign policy stand as premier evils today, you will probably think the dominant applications worked out in this book are wise and even prophetic; if instead you think that both globalization and current American foreign policy are mixed bags, you will probably find this book over the top or even a bit silly at times. But it is a great read.

Gordon H. Clark (/Presbyterian & Reformed 1989, $6.95) oscillates between the insightful and the ill-informed. *William Hendriksen* (NTC; 1979) has already been mentioned under Philippians. The ET of the exposition by *Jean Daillé* [b. 1594 in France] produced by Klock and Klock (1983) is now out of print; the commentary by *John Eadie* is back in print (/Wipf & Stock 1998, $26.00). The very substantial work of *John Davenant*, whose Latin original first appeared in 1627, was translated into English in 1831—and that translation has just been reprinted (two volumes in one; /BoT 2005, £19.00/$35.00). The expository commentary by *Charles Erdman*, one-time Professor of Practical Theology at Princeton Seminary, is again out of print. *H. C. G. Moule* is as useful here as anywhere as a supplement to a more substantial commentary (reprint, /Kregel 1982, $6.99). *Patrick V. Rogers* (NTM; 1981, £1.00/op) adds little. The BST contribution by R. C. Lucas, *Fullness and*

119

Freedom (1984, £9.99/$15.00), is worth scanning; there is then little
need to read Thomas Trevethan, *Our Joyful Confidence: The Lordship
of Christ in Colossians* (1981, op). Some practical advice is found in *S.
Cox and A. H. Drysdale* on Philemon ([1897], recently reprinted by
/Klock and Klock 1982, but again op)—not so much a commentary as
a series of lectures on ministry and some notes. The EBC contribution
on Colossians is by *Curtis Vaughan* (see Ephesians for details). It is clear
and straightforward but adds little to the major volumes. *Arthur A.
Rupprecht* has contributed the Philemon comments in the same volume.
One of the better expositions is that of *R. Kent Hughes* (/Crossway
1989, $21.99). Other works at the popular end of the scale include
Roy Yates (Epworth 1993, £6.95/) and *John MacArthur* (Moody 1995,
£14.25/1992, $22.99).

3.14 Thessalonians

The best all-round commentary on the Greek text of these epistles is
that of *Charles A. Wanamaker* (NIGTC; 1990, £29.99/$40.00). Wana-
maker is thorough and usually sensitive to both literary and theological
flow. For students and pastors who can handle Greek, this commentary
falls into the "must" column. His handling of the rhetorical elements of
the epistle, though, is sometimes overdone. A little more accessible is the
WBC volume by *F. F. Bruce* (1986, £19.99/$39.99). Characterized by
Bruce's thoroughness and care for detail, the work is especially valuable
in its introductory remarks, its careful delineation of the background,
and its useful excursus on "The Antichrist." Richer on the Greco-Roman
background and its bearing on the interpretation of these two epistles is
the work of *Abraham Malherbe* (AB; 2000, op/$50.00). Occasionally
one wants to remind the author that background information must not
be a substitute for penetrating theological understanding. *Gene Green*
(Pillar; 2002, £28.99/$42.00) displays similar strengths in the Hellenistic
context, but preserves a better balance of strengths, making it a very useful volume for pastors and students. A standard is the BNTC/HNTC
volume by *Ernest Best* (Black 1972, op/reprint, Hendrickson 1995,
$29.95), which is thorough and moderately conservative in most of its

conclusions. No less competent is the work by *I. Howard Marshall* (NCB; 1983/$17.00), which tends to build on the work by Best and carry the discussion through the literature published since Best's commentary appeared. It is therefore wise to read Marshall in conjunction with Best. Marshall replaces the earlier NCB volume by *Arthur L. Moore*, which was adequate and helpful within its space limitations but far too brief to be a first choice. The SP volume by *Earl Richard* (1995, £26.99/$34.95) is clear and focused on philology. It adopts many interesting positions, some of them plausible, some of them implausible. Richard argues that 1 Thessalonians is earlier (mid-40s) than most people think, but holds that it is a composite of an earlier missive (2:13–4:2), full of joy, inserted into a later one (1:1–2:12 + 4:3–5:28) written to respond to specific concerns. Further, 2:14–16 constitutes a further interpolation, and 2:13 and the first part of 3:11 are redactional comments. In line with much contemporary scholarship, he thinks that the literary, theological, and sociological problems of 2 Thessalonians can be untangled only by subscribing to a theory of pseudonymity. See the insightful review by A. D. Weima in *JBL* 116 (1997): 761–63.

Too brief to be a first choice, but a sensible work within its limitations, is the work of *David John Williams* (NIBC; 1992, op/$14.95). *Jacob W. Elias* (BCBC; 1995, £13.75/$24.99) is accessible but not penetrating; the same must be said of *Michael D. Martin* (AC; 1995, $29.99). The NIVAC entry is by *Michael Holmes* (/1998, $21.99). The Interpretation volume by *Beverly Roberts Gaventa* (/1998, £14.99/$24.95) is slender in both volume and substance.

Leon Morris has contributed two commentaries on these epistles and has revised both of them. His contribution to the NIC series (/1994, $32.00) tends virtually to eclipse his entry in the TNTC series (1985, £9.99/$14.00). He has also now added the Word Biblical Themes volume to his treatment of these epistles (1989, $9.99). *Robert L. Thomas* (EBC; now in paperback, bound with the Pastorals; Hodder 1996, op/Zondervan, $15.99) is determinedly exegetical but somehow manages to detect pretribulational dispensationalism where many of his readers will not find it. Something similar could be said for *D. Edmond Hiebert* (rev. ed.; Moody 1995, op), though this one is written with more warmth. *Earl Palmer* has provided a rather weak contribution to the GNC series (1985, op); this one was never transmuted into NIBC since it was simply replaced by Williams (see above). *R. A. Ward* (1974, op) is a fine supplemental commentary for pastors, but it should be used in conjunction with a more detailed work. *Ernest W. Saunders* (KPG; on Thessalonians, Philippians, and Philemon; 1981, /$4.95) is one of the better entries in the series though clearly hampered by brevity. *D. E. H. Whiteley* (NClar; 1969, op) is a small but useful supplement. *William Neil* (Moffatt; op) is worth scanning but is showing signs of age. In the British edition, *W. Hendriksen*'s commentary is bound with his work on the Pastorals (NTC; BoT 1983, £19.95); in the American edition, it is bound with his work on Hebrews (Baker 1996, $49.99). The commentary by *Kenneth Grayston* was mentioned under Philippians. *Gary W. Demarest* has produced the CC entry on Thessalonians and the Pastorals (/Thomas Nelson 2003, $16.99), and it is a fairly strong entry in a weak series. Perhaps the best of the popular treatments is the BST commentary by *John R. W. Stott* (1994, $15.00), with *David Jackman* (Christian Focus 1998, /$12.99) not far behind. Other popular works include *J. P. Arthur* (Evangelical Press 1996, £7.95/); *David P. Kuske* (Concordia 1994, /$7.99); *Frederick A. Tatford* (J. Richie 1991, £8.95/Loizeaux Brothers, $14.99); and *Jon Weatherly* (College Press 1996, $26.99). The volume by *Knute Larson*, covering not only the Thessalonian epistles but also the Pastorals and Philemon, is cast at the elementary level typical of its series (/HNTC; Broadman & Holman 2000, $19.99). The New Testament Readings volume by *Martin J. J. Menken* (Routledge 1994, £57.50 hb or £17.99 pb/$99.94 hb or $30.95 pb) manages to be simultaneously short, eccentric, and expensive.

Among older works, *James Denney* (EB; op) will make a good secondhand supplement, though it is insufficient on its own. *James Moffatt* (EGT; 5 vols.; /Eerdmans, op) can still be useful. *G. Milligan* in the older Macmillan series on the Greek text (i.e., comparable to Swete on Mark or Creed on Luke) has been reprinted (/Kregel 1986, $12.99) and is worth reading even though in some respects it is terribly dated. *E. J. Bicknell* (WC; op) is of indifferent value; *J. E. Frame* (ICC; 1912, £40.00/$39.95) is not much better. *C. F. Hogg and W. E. Vine* produced a very simple commentary rather like Tenney on John but with occasionally useful comments on individual words, and it has come back into print (Word Entertainment 1997, £12.99/Thomas Nelson, $14.99). The Baker reprint of the exposition of *Charles Erdman* is out of print.

Specialists will want to read Charles H. Giblin, *The Threat to Faith* (1967, op), a detailed examination of 2 Thessalonians 2 and its relation to apocalyptic. Two "commentaries" that are not really commentaries will also draw their interest. Abraham Malherbe, *Paul and the Thessalonians: The Philosophic Tradition of Pastoral Care* (Fortress 1987, op/$12.00), draws many interesting Greco-Roman parallels to Paul's approach to pastoral care in the Thessalonian letters. But Malherbe does not adequately work out the fundamental differences that arise from Paul's eschatological vision. Robert Jewett, *The Thessalonian Correspondence: Pauline Rhetoric and Millenarian Piety* (Fortress 1986, op) develops sociological categories to explain Pauline rhetoric. By focusing so narrowly, both Malherbe and Jewett have shed a little fresh insight; by the same token, their studies seem rather reductionistic. The volume of essays edited by Karl Donfried and Johannes Beutler, *The Thessalonians Debate* (/Eerdmans 2000, $25.00), provides an up-to-date state of play on many aspects of Thessalonians study. Advanced students will be grateful for A. D. Weima and Stanley E. Porter, *An Annotated Bibliography of 1 and 2 Thessalonians* (New Testament Studies and Tools 26; Brill 1998, /$121.00). One should not overlook access to patristic thought in the ACCS volume by *Peter Gorday* (see above on Colossians).

3.15 Pastorals

A couple of decades ago, these epistles were not well served by commentaries in English, but this has changed. The NIGTC commentary by *George W. Knight III* (1992, £39.99/$50.00) lies in the "must" column. It is cautious, conservative, and thoughtful. Over 850 pages in length, the new ICC commentary by *I. Howard Marshall* (1999, £55.00 hb/$95.00 hb; 2004, £19.99 pb/$39.95 pb) is packed with thoughtful, well-written reflection on every issue of importance, but many readers will think that some of the interpretations are being skewed by Marshall's view that these epistles were not written by Paul. The contribution of *William D. Mounce* (/WBC; 2000, $30.00) is something of a foil to Marshall: he is more conservative than Marshall (for instance, on the question of authorship), though not, in general, quite as penetrating. Moreover, your sanctification must endure the irritating format of this series. The AB volume on Titus alone, by *J. D. Quinn* (1990, $28.00), is also full of really excellent exegesis, even though he thinks that the Pastoral Epistles "as we have them" probably stem from AD 80–85. The complementary AB volume on 1 and 2 Timothy is by *Luke Timothy Johnson* (/2001, $40.00), and, as usual, what he has written is well worth reading. *J. D. Quinn and William C. Wacker*, on 1 and 2 Timothy, display the same tradition of meticulous mainstream scholarship in their very recent ECC volume (2000, £37.99/$65.00), with full consideration of the historical, literary, and social contexts (which are, inevitably, tied to judgments about authorship and date). The volume by *Raymond F. Collins* (NTLNTM; Westminster John Knox 2002, £30.00/$34.95) is substantial and worth reading but suffers a bit when it is compared with some of the works just mentioned. *Walter L. Liefeld* (/NIVAC; 1999, $24.99) is lighter yet and so cautious that it somehow misses the fire of these epistles.

In the past, the standard work most cited by scholars was *H. Conzelmann and M. Dibelius*, available in English in the Hermeneia series (1972, £21.99/$38.00). But the work has now been superseded by the commentaries just listed and in any case was always somewhat overrated. It was far too committed to an unbelievable reconstruction of early church history to be very useful to most pastors. *J. N. D. Kelly* (BNTC/HNTC; 1993, £19.99 pb/$24.95 hb) provides a useful all-round commentary, including some brief comments about the more naive assumptions that sometimes underlie computer criticism. One of the better commentaries is that by *Gordon D. Fee*, both in its GNC form (1984, op) and in its NIBC metamorphosis (7th ed.; 2000, £11.99/$14.95). Despite a number of points where I find his exegesis unsatisfying, Fee has worked hard at building a more or less believable "life setting" that ties the contents of these three epistles together. The *Thomas D. Lea* volume for NAC (/1992, $29.99) is competent but a bit bland. Do not overlook the relatively brief commentary by *Philip Towner* in the

IVPNTC (1994, £9.99/$20.00), for it represents the condensation of years of serious study of these epistles. The volume in the New Testament in Context series (1996, £15.99/$20.00) finds *Luke Timothy Johnson* at his best: for its length, the work is both a model of clarity and packed with useful information. His KPG volume (see below) is probably unnecessary if you have this one, and this one may not be necessary if you have his AB volume (see above)!

Daniel C. Arichea has produced the UBS Handbook on the Pastoral Epistles (/1995, $24.95), *Jouette Bassler* the ANTC entry (1996, £12.99/$21.00)—not noteworthy, and with a marked tendency to dance to agendas other than Paul's—and *Margaret Davies* both the NTG "guide" (1996, op/$15.95) and the slim Epworth commentary (1996, £8.95/$13.50), neither worth buying.

J. L. Houlden's earlier Pelican commentary (1976, op) has now been revised and placed in another series (TPINT; 1989, £6.50 pb/$15.00) and is worth perusing. *C. K. Barrett* (NClar; 1963, op) packs much material into little space. *Reginald H. Fuller* (ProcC; with J. Paul Sampley on Ephesians, other authors on Colossians and 2 Thessalonians; 1978, op) is praised by some, but he is so tied to a late date and situation that all his exegesis is affected. *Donald Guthrie*, now in the revised edition (TNTC; 1990, £9.99/$14.00), has become something of a classic not least because of its introduction and defense of Pauline authorship, but preachers will wish he had been given more space to erect an exegetical foundation and to locate the epistles in some focused situation. *Walter Lock* (ICC; 1928, £35.00 pb/op) is now hopelessly dated but contains a number of perennially relevant observations. *Luke Timothy Johnson* (KPG; 1987, op) is one of the better ones in the series, but see his work in the AB series (above). *Thomas C. Oden* (Interpretation; Westminster John Knox 1989, £17.99/$24.95) is a remarkable work—well written and defending Pauline authorship. But it is not a traditional commentary: it organizes the pericopae topically, with the preacher in mind. This makes it harder to follow the flow of the text but has some advantages for the preacher who is trying to group together some of the material Paul treats.

A. T. Hanson followed his brief commentary (CBC; 1966, op) with a larger one (NCB; 1982, op) and with some longer discussions in

Studies in the Pastoral Epistles (1968, op). This concentrates on difficult passages, and the author often has some fresh suggestions to make, but the best of these have now been culled by the more recent commentaries. Not a commentary, but no less useful, is the brief study by George W. Knight III, *The Faithful Sayings in the Pastoral Epistles* (op). Access to patristic comment in the ACCS series can be found in *Gorday* (above, on Colossians). *E. K. Simpson* (op) on the Greek text has valuable linguistic comments and numerous parallels, but the commentary is stodgy and fails to grapple with the theological thrusts of these epistles. Some find help in *W. Hendriksen* (NTC; see above under Thessalonians). *R. A. Ward* (1974, op) is worth scanning but is not a first choice. He preserves some useful insights for the preacher. Similarly undistinguished but from a less conservative perspective is the commentary by *Arland J. Hultgren and Roger Aus* (ACNT; 1984, £10.99 pb/$17.25 pb), which strangely lumps together the Pastoral Epistles and 2 Thessalonians. *Robert J. Karris* does not show off the NTM series at its best (1980, op). The EBC divides the Pastorals: 1 and 2 Timothy are treated by *Ralph Earle*, and Titus by *D. Edmond Hiebert* (details in notes on Ephesians). These may be worth a fast skim, but they do not make up in quality what they necessarily lose in brevity. *James D. G. Dunn* covers these three epistles in brief compass in the NIB (vol. 12; Abingdon 1998, $60.00).

Popular works abound, of which I mention only a handful. *H. C. G. Moule* on 2 Timothy has been reprinted (/Kregel 1981, $10.99), but this work sometimes moves from the devotional to the sentimental and is not one of Moule's better books. John R. W. Stott's *Guard the Gospel*—on 2 Timothy (BST; 1984, £8.99/$15.00)—is certainly worth reading and has now been supplemented by his *Guard the Truth*, on 1 Timothy and Titus, for the same series (BST; 1996, £9.99/$17.99). *Gareth L. Reese* (College Press 1990, op) is long (almost 600 pages) and rather verbose. It is cast at a popular level, but the length cuts against that level. Also worth reading are *Douglas Milne* (/FoB; 1996, $10.99) and *Michael Bentley* in the Welwyn Commentary (Evangelical Press 1997, £9.95/). Less urgent are *Bruce B. Barton* in the Life Application series (/1993, $14.99); *Michael Griffiths* (Crossway 1996, £4.99/Baker 1996, $9.99);

C. Michael Moss (/College Press 1995, $19.99); and *John MacArthur* on 1 Timothy (/Moody 1995, $23.99).

Indispensable for those who can cope with French is the fourth edition of the two-volume commentary (898 pp.) by *Ceslaus Spicq* (EtBib; 1969).

Three of the reprints I mentioned in the third edition of this *Survey*—viz. *Patrick Fairbairn*, orig. 1874; *Charles Erdman*; and *Henry P. Liddon* on 1 Timothy—are again out of print. On the other hand, *John Calvin*, now condensed and modernized for the Crossway Classic Commentaries (/Crossway 1998, $14.99) is well worth buying and perusing.

3.16 Hebrews

The last two or three decades have treated Hebrews to several magnificent commentaries. *Harold W. Attridge* (Hermeneia; 1989, £28.99 pb/$50.00 hb), on the Greek text, is masterful. Here and there it may tilt a little too far toward Greco-Roman parallels at the expense of Jewish sources, but no serious student of the text can afford to ignore this commentary. Equally impressive is the commentary by *Paul Ellingworth* (NIGTC; 1993, £39.99/$60.00). It is stronger in analyzing the subtleties of the Greek text. (If you buy this commentary, you do not need his Handbook in the UBS series [/1994, $24.99] unless you are a Bible translator.) The commentary by *William Lane* (WBC; 2 vols.; 1991, £19.99/$39.99 each), however, is a little more accessible to students and pastors whose Greek is weak than are the Attridge and Ellingworth volumes. Moreover, Lane often provides a better mix of technical comment and thoughtful theology. Lane's popular-level *Call to Commitment: Responding to the Message of Hebrews* (Hendrickson 1985; reprint Regent College 2004, £14.00 pb/$18.95 pb) you can circulate around the congregation while you are expounding the text in more detail. The NCB volume by *Robert McLachlan Wilson* (1987, op) is competent and interesting in its own way but is now outstripped by Lane, Ellingworth, and Attridge. The NIVAC contribution by *George Guthrie* (/1998, £16.99/$27.99) is above average for the series: Guthrie has been working on this epistle for a long time. The Interpretation volume by *Thomas G.*

Long (1997, £14.99/$24.05) is sometimes creative, but not disciplined and too brief to be of primary help. The recent one by David deSilva, with the title *Perseverance in Gratitude* (Eerdmans 2000, £22.99/$40.00), is well written (that is always the case with deSilva) but so focuses on the themes indicated by the title that the commentary seems to skirt over the fundamental theological, Christological, and canonical realities that, Hebrews insists, constitute the *reasons why* Christians ought to "persevere in gratitude." The contribution of *Craig R. Koester* (AB; 2001, strangely op) is far stronger; I am not sure why it has not received wider notice. The commentary by *Gareth Cockerill*, in the Wesleyan tradition, is undistinguished (/Wesleyan 1999, $24.95). The work of *Peter O'Brien* is slated to appear in due course in the Pillar series.

Until this latest string of commentaries appeared, the two best English works on Hebrews were doubtless those of *F. F. Bruce* (/NIC; rev. ed.; 1997, /$38.00) and *Philip E. Hughes* (Eerdmans 1987, op/$55.00). In some ways the two commentaries complement each other. Bruce provides a great deal of useful exegetical information and writes with caution, but this new revised edition is changed so little from his first edition (1964) that if you already have the first there is little point in purchasing the second. In any case, Lane is now to be preferred. The commentary by Hughes focuses less attention on lexical matters and contemporary secondary literature, but it is better than most modern commentaries at surveying the history of interpretation across the entire span of the church, not just the last few decades or centuries. It certainly wrestles with theological questions more thoroughly than does the work by Bruce.

The commentary by *H. Montefiore*, published in the same year as the first edition of Bruce (BNTC/HNTC; 1964, £19.99/$19.95), is stimulating and provocative but not particularly useful or reliable. At one level, none of these commentaries completely overshadows, for the preacher, *William Barclay* (DSB; rev. ed.; St Andrew/Westminster 1976, £6.50 pb/$29.95 hb or $14.95 pb). Elsewhere Barclay confesses that Hebrews is one of his favorite parts of Scripture, and here he expounds it quite brilliantly, always revealing the practical message of the chapters but showing more intimacy between Hebrews and Philo than is really warranted. Also worth reading is *Donald A. Hagner* (GNC; op; precursor to /NIBC; Paternoster 1990, £11.99/Hendrickson 1990, $14.95), though it adds little to the ones already mentioned. Of much less value is the small commentary by *Robert H. Smith* (/Abingdon 1994, $21.00), now eclipsed by *Victor C. Pfitzner* (/ACNT; 1997, $21.00).

For students with the necessary languages, it is essential to explore the Greek text with the French two-volume work by *Ceslaus Spicq* (CNT; 1977)—though he makes Philo more important than he really is—and the German commentary by *Hans-Friedrich Weiss* (KEK; 1991).

G. W. Buchanan (/AB; 1972, $29.00) is a rather strange and off-beat commentary. It sees Messiahship in Hebrews in political terms and the "rest" as entry into the physical land. *F. J. Schierse* (bound with Thessalonians and James; Sheed and Ward, £7.00/) sometimes has fresh ways of putting the argument in Hebrews but is too brief to add much to the larger works. *James Moffatt* (ICC; 1924, £35.00/$69.95), although hardly worth its normal price now that Attridge and Ellingworth have appeared, remains nevertheless a work of considerable learning and can often be picked up secondhand. *B. F. Westcott* (op) was doubtless indispensable in its day but has now been culled by the best recent works. A. Nairne, *The Epistle of Priesthood* (CUP 1921, op), consists of a brief commentary with a very long introduction of some three hundred pages. Perhaps its chief value is that of explaining the older "sacramental principle" type of theology. *T. Hewitt* (TNTC; op) was one of the weakest entries in the old series and has now been replaced in the new TNTC series by the sturdy work of *Donald Guthrie* (1983, £9.99/1994, $14.00). Thoroughly unrewarding is the work by *Theodore H. Robinson* (Moffatt; op). For the commentary by *Simon J. Kistemaker*, see §1.4. *Leon Morris* (EBC 12, running to Revelation; 1981) is worth skimming, but he has not given us his best work. He is entirely eclipsed by *R. T. France* in the new edition of EBC (EBC 13, running from Hebrews to Revelation; 2006, $39.99). *Paul Ellingworth* (Epworth 1991, £6.95/$9.95 pb) is a useful short commentary, but it usually sheds more light on the use of the language than on the flow of the thought or the theology of the epistle: skip it and buy the impressive NIGTC volume (see above). Weighed by the accuracy of its exegesis, the IVPNTC entry by *Ray Stedman* (1991,

£9.99/$20.00) is a weak entry in the series. *James Girdwood* (/College Press 1997, $32.99) is no better.

F. V. Filson's study *Yesterday* (op) aims to shed fresh light on the epistle by viewing it from the vantage point of chapter 13. Among other things, it rightly warns against a platonic interpretation of the "unchanging" Christ. An excellent if somewhat verbose and diffuse rebuttal of the position that sees many philonic categories in Hebrews is Ronald Williamson's *Philo and the Epistle to the Hebrews* (Brill 1970, op). Though dated, it is still worth scanning. W. Manson's study (not commentary), *The Epistle to the Hebrews* (1951, op), is sometimes illuminating, especially in relation to Acts 7, but, like all works on Hebrews published before the availability of the Qumran scrolls, it is divorced from modern discussion. The use of the OT at Qumran, for instance, has at least some bearing on the use of the OT in Hebrews. Not surprisingly 11QMelch has provoked a long list of studies on how Melchizedek is handled in Jewish exegesis, the most important of which is perhaps Fred L. Horton, *The Melchizedek Tradition* (SNTSMS 30; 1976, op). Another major study in the same series that repays close reading is the book by David Peterson, *Hebrews and Perfection* (SNTSMS 47; 1982, op). Anyone who wrestles with the way Hebrews is put together might well read George Guthrie, *The Structure of Hebrews: A Text-Linguistic Approach* (reprint, /Baker 1998, $22.99 [originally published by Brill in 1994]). "Text-Linguistics" is simply another label for discourse analysis. Now dated but still stimulating is the provocative work by Ernst Käsemann, *The Wandering People of God* (Augsburg 1984, op). This was written in a period of imprisonment under the Nazis in 1937, when Käsemann was identifying the German radical Confessing Church with the church in Hebrews, understood as the new people of God in its wandering through the wilderness, following the Pioneer and Perfecter of faith. Many of the history-of-religions presuppositions in the work have been eclipsed, and numerous details of exegesis may be questioned. Nevertheless, the work is almost as thought-provoking today as when it appeared. Several recent treatments of the "new covenant" theme have appeared, the most important of which is probably that of Susanne Lehne, *The New Covenant in Hebrews* (JSOT 1990, £50.00/$74.00). In one of the last publications before his death, Barnabas Lindars gave us *The Theology of the Letter to the Hebrews* (NTT; CUP 1991, £13.99 pb/$20.99 pb). Not only scholars but also preachers may well appreciate the critical edition of an old classic by William Perkins, *A Commentary on Hebrews 11* (/Pilgrim [1609] 1991, $39.95 hb or $29.95 pb). Assistance with the patristic sources is found in the ACCS volume by *Erik Heen* and *D. W. Philip* (/2005, $40.00). The volume by *R. P. Gordon* in the Readings series (SAP 2000, £16.99/$37.95 hb or $32.95 pb) is very good within the limitations of its length but over-priced. The inexperienced preacher who is first trying to break into Hebrews might consider reading Andrew H. Trotter, *Interpreting the Epistle to the Hebrews* (/Baker 1997, $16.99).

At the popular and sometimes devotional level, one may still purchase the much reprinted work by Andrew Murray, *The Holiest of All* (/Whitaker House 2004, $17.99). Despite (or perhaps because of) the doctrinal bias toward "higher life" tradition, the book remains a collection of marvelously pious and spiritually-minded gems strung out on a string of abysmal exegesis. More accurate by far is the BST contribution by *Raymond E. Brown* (1984, £9.99/$15.00). Not to be overlooked is the little work by Robert Jewett, *Letter to Pilgrims* (/Pilgrim 1981, op). Jewett did his doctoral study on Hebrews, so he has thought long and hard over this epistle, and there is often depth in the comments. Occasionally the agenda determines the exegesis, but the work contains some useful reflections on suffering. The old standbys of *H. C. G. Moule* (reprint, /Kregel 1998, $5.99) and *Charles Erdman* (reprint, /Evangelical Literature League 1987, op) are worth a quick skim. *Louis H. Evans Jr.* (CC; 1986, £12.99/1991, $10.99 pb) is warm but thin; *Rea McDonnell* (MBS; 1991, £7.25/Liturgical 1986, $12.95 hb or $7.95 pb) is very thin; so also is the WBComp entry on Hebrews and James by *Frances Taylor Gench* (1996, £9.99/$19.95). Considerably better is the volume by *Jerry Vines* (/Loizeaux 1993, $14.99). Surprisingly good is a rather large volume by *Gareth L. Reese* (Scripture Exposition Books; College Press 1992, op). Clearly designed for theological students and fledgling preachers, the book is written with admirable clarity and a winning ability to cut to the heart of a lot of issues. The twenty-eight-page appendix on covenants and various forms of covenant theology may not win universal agreement, but it is fair and informed. Normally I would be suspicious of a further thirty-five-page appendix offering suggested sermon outlines, but these are surprisingly good. The work by *R. Kent Hughes* (2 vols.; /Crossway 1993, $21.99 each—though only the first volume seems to be in print at the moment) shows how to move from text to sermon. There are many other popular treatments, but the busy pastor or student can afford to give most of them a miss.

The epistle to the Hebrews seems to be a fertile ground for stimulating the reprinting of old commentaries. Of less interest, except to the specialist in the study of Hebrews, are: Robert Anderson, *Types in Hebrews* (/Kregel 1978, $11.99 pb); *A. B. Bruce* (/Kregel nd, op); E. W. Bullinger, *Great Cloud of Witnesses in Hebrews Eleven* (/Kregel [1911] 1986, $18.99 pb); *Thomas C. Edwards* (/Kregel [1911] nd, op); and *Adolph Saphir* (2 vols. in 1; /Kregel [1875] 1983, $24.99). The reprint, three volumes in one, of *William Goudge* (/Kregel [1866] nd) is now itself out of print. On the other hand, an older work that is still worth a close reading is the two-volume commentary by *Franz Delitzsch*, now regrettably op. *John Owen*'s work has been condensed and modernized for the Crossway Classic Commentaries series (/Crossway 1998, $15.99). John Calvin's *Sermons on Melchizedek and Abraham*, which first appeared in English in 1592, have been reprinted (Old Paths 2000, but again op).

3.17 James

The five recent large-scale English commentaries on James are by *Peter H. Davids* (NIGTC; 1982, £29.99/$35.00); *Sophie Laws* (BNTC/HNTC; 1980, £19.99/1993, $24.95); *Ralph P. Martin* (WBC; 1988, £19.99/$39.99); *Luke Timothy Johnson* (AB; 1995, op/$45.00); and *Douglas J. Moo* (Pillar; 2000, /$30.00). Davids is on the Greek text in Greek font; the latter two can more easily be read by a wider audience. Davids places James in a setting of Jewish messianists in the 50s and 60s; Laws lays out the possibility of a Roman provenance; Martin is a masterpiece of condensed writing and an admirable summary of the current status of scholarship on James, but I find myself wanting to qualify his judgments often enough that it is not my first choice. Johnson is superb on introductory matters, including an excellent forty-page survey of the history of the interpretation of this book and a thought-provoking assessment of the relationships this book properly has with the thought of the rest of the New Testament, including Paul. (Johnson thinks that neither Paul nor James was using or confronting the other, and that both have much more in common than is usually recognized, once we free James to be "read in terms of 108 verses rather than 12 verses.") Johnson is always incisive, though I am less persuaded by some of his exegetical decisions than by those in the next commentary. Moo's work (not to be confused with his TNTC contribution, below), though not as long as the other four, is a lovely blend of good judgment, good writing, good theology, and sometimes good application.

Two other recent works deserve comment. *Robert Wall* (TPI 1997, £16.99/$29.95) offers a "canonical reading" of James. He "focuses more narrowly on the literary texture and theological subject matter of the canonical James than on the ancient social and literary environs that produced it" (p. 1). But there are different kinds of "canonical readings," of course. What Wall does not set out to do is show how James contributes to a unified and richly-layered canonical-theological structure; rather, his purpose is to locate this letter among the varieties of theology and practice that characterized first-century Christianity. He is interested in the role of this epistle in the larger canonical discussion of the significance of the life and ministry of Jesus. Randall C. Webber provides a *Reader Response Analysis of the Epistle of James* (International Scholars Publication 1996, £60.50 hb or £44.45 pb/$75.50 hb or $53.95 pb), outrageously priced for a 125-page paperback. It is interesting enough, and, reader-response jargon aside, it is clearly written. Its most significant weakness is that it is so keen on polyvalent readings that it offers no programmatic help on how such readings may or may not be warranted. The work by Richard Bauckham, *James: Wisdom of James, Disciple of Jesus*, in the New Testament Readings series (1999, £65 hb or £20.99 pb/$125.00 hb or $38.95 pb), is equally outrageous in price but superb in substance; use a library.

The German commentary by *M. Dibelius* (1928) was revised by *H. Greeven* (1964) and translated to become the entry in the Hermeneia

NEW TESTAMENT COMMENTARY SURVEY

series (1976, £27.99/1972, $55.00). Its chief value is the systematic attempt to compare the epistle with other pieces of hortatory literature. Preachers who can cope with Greek may also wish to consult the old standard by *J. B. Mayor* (reprint, /Kregel 1990, $32.99 hb or $26.99 pb), originally part of the older Macmillan series. The thoroughness of Mayor's work is quite breathtaking, but he is not always as helpful on the practical side as one might desire. The old ICC contributions of *F. J. A. Hort* (1909, as far as 4:7; op) and *John H. Ropes* (1924, £35.00/$75.00) are useful for their classical and Hellenistic parallels. The standard German entry is by *F. Mussner* (3rd ed.; Herder 1975).

C. L. Mitton has written a fine commentary combining scholarly exegesis and practical insight (1966; unfortunately op). The balance is wholly admirable; many other writers are too often content with lame paraphrases of the text. In the same class is the new TNTC contribution by *Douglas J. Moo* (1986, £9.99/1987, $14.00). The older and much slimmer TNTC volume was by *R. V. G. Tasker* (1957, op). *Peter H. Davids*, in his contribution to NIBC (1989, £11.99/$14.95 pb), has given us a slimmer and less technical commentary than the one he prepared for NIGTC. Those who can work with Greek should buy his NIGTC; those who can't, his NIBC. There is no need to buy both. *Gerald Bray* provides access to patristic comment in the ACCS series (/2000, $40.00)—covering also 1–2 Peter, 1–3 John, and Jude. The ANTC entry by *C. Freeman Sleeper* (/1998, $20.00) is weak. The original NIC contribution was that of *Alexander Ross* (1954, op), a book warmly devotional in tone but offering no serious help in the difficult passages. It was replaced by *J. Adamson* (/1976, $32.00), a book somewhat dated even when it appeared and disproportionately dependent on Hellenistic parallels at the expense of Jewish sources. Adamson has superseded his own work in his volume *James: The Man and His Message* (/Eerdmans 1989, op). The EBC volume by *Donald W. Burdick* (vol. 12—see on Hebrews; 1981) is unremarkable; far better is the revised EBC work of *George Guthrie* (vol. 13—see on Hebrews; 2006). Singularly poor at the level of exegesis (which must be the first concern of the commentator) are both *Kurt Richardson* (/NAC; 1997, $29.99) and *David P. Nystrom* in the NIVAC series (/1997, $22.99). Only somewhat better is *George M. Stulac* (IVPNTC; £9.99/$14.99).

J. Moffatt (Moffatt; bound with Peter and Jude; 1928, op) sheds some light on the background but has now been superseded. *E. M. Sidebottom* (NCB, with 2 Peter and Jude; 1982, op/Attic 1967, $7.50 or Eerdmans 1982, op) is disappointing and very thin where comment is most needed. *Bo Reicke* (/AB, with Peter and Jude; 2nd ed.; 1964, $18.00 pb) is somewhat better but now eclipsed by Davids, Laws, and Moo. In any case, the early volumes of AB are being replaced and expanded: cf. Luke Timothy Johnson's AB volume on James alone (noted above).

I have not usually mentioned the Helps for Translators series put out by UBS because most of the volumes, though doubtless helpful to translators, are so thin on background and theology that they are of minimal use to students and preachers. But *Robert G. Bratcher* on James, Peter, and Jude (1983, op) offers good value for the money. So also does *J. Harold Greenlee* in his Exegetical Summary (SIL 1993, op). The CC commentary by *Paul A. Cedar* on James, 1 and 2 Peter, and Jude (/1984, $24.99) offers application but little exegesis; even in the former, Mitton is usually more incisive.

Understandably, popular commentaries on James abound. On this book, they are distractions unless one has first engaged in careful exegesis. I mention only a handful. *Curtis Vaughan* (/Zondervan nd, $6.99 pb) is worth scanning; *Richard Kugelman* (NTM; 1981, £6.95/$5.95) just barely. *R. A. Martin and John H. Elliott* (ACNT on James, 1 and 2 Peter, and Jude; 1982, £10.99/$17.25) offers competent digests of exegeses but is too brief to be very helpful and sometimes too speculative to be very convincing. *D. Edmond Hiebert* (/Moody 1992, £13.50/op) is a bit stodgy but worth skimming. *Zane C. Hodges* (/Grace Evangelical Society 1994, $11.99) adds little to more substantial works except the dubious slant of his theological agenda. The Interpretation volume by *Pheme Perkins* covers James, 1 and 2 Peter, and Jude (/1995, $24.95). *R. Kent Hughes* (/Crossway 1991, $21.99) takes us from text to sermon; *John MacArthur* (/Moody 1998, $23.99) straddles the fence. The exposition by *J. Alec Motyer* (BST; 1985, £9.99/1988, $15.00) displays the strengths we have come to expect from this series, along with some thoughtful suggestions as to the structure of James.

Useful reprints in addition to those already mentioned include the commentary by *Robert Johnstone* (reprint, BoT 1977, op), the expository lectures from the last century by *Rudolf E. Stier* (/Kregel [1871] 1982, op), and *Thomas Manton's* classic, available both from BoT (1968, £11.95 hb) and Crossway (1995, £9.99 pb/$19.99).

3.18 1 Peter

Except in a couple of instances, I shall not mention commentaries incorporated with James.

The fullest commentary in English at the exegetical level is that of *Paul J. Achtemeier* (/Hermeneia; 1996, $50.00). It is a masterpiece of careful scholarship. The parallels are full but not intrusive. Achtemeier has a knack for getting to the heart of an issue quickly, while his footnotes allow more advanced readers to pursue fine points. The writing is clear, and much of the exegesis admirable. Nevertheless, he tentatively holds that the epistle is pseudonymous, opting for a date in the 80s or 90s. His exegesis at a few critical points (e.g., 2:13) strikes me as being far more controlled by contemporary agendas than is warranted by accurate handling of the text. Nevertheless, it is much stronger than another one of similar length—the AB commentary by *John H. Elliott* (2000, op/$60.00), which is so controlled by Elliott's "home for the homeless" thesis (see below) that most of the vision is driven by social-science perspectives. In some ways the best general-use commentary on 1 Peter is now that of *Karen Jobes* (/BECNT; 2005, $39.95). This work is strong on every front while remaining accessible. It deserves wide circulation.

J. Ramsey Michaels (WBC; 1988, £19.99/$39.99) is scarcely less important. Michaels tentatively dates this epistle to the last quarter of the first century; occasionally this affects his exegesis. Michaels has also contributed the Word Biblical Themes volume (1989, np). *Donald Senior* (on 1 and 2 Peter and Jude) is useful but cannot compete with the larger works (/SP; 2003, $39.95). The contribution of *M. Eugene Boring* (ANTC; 1999, £11.99/$20.00) is (as is common with this author) rather inventive. Boring argues that 1 Peter is pseudonymous and an amalgam of Petrine and Pauline tradition (shades of the old-fashioned Tübingen School; when will scholars get over it?). But Appendix A on the narrative world of 1 Peter is almost worth the price of the entire volume. Rather distinctive is the volume by *Donald G. Miller* (/Pickwick 1993, $30.00). It is clearly designed for the pastor: although the author is obviously familiar with a wide range of views and quotes others frequently, he never acknowledges the source and does not identify who holds to various positions. There are fresh applications at many points, without this being in any sense a "devotional" commentary. But it makes more than its share of exegetical and grammatical mistakes and cannot be considered a first choice, though it would make excellent supplementary reading. *Peter Davids* (NIC; 1995, £19.99/$34.00) is competent and clear. Granted the limitations of the series, *I. Howard Marshall* in the IVPNTC series (1990, £9.99/$20.00) is superb. Unlike some volumes in the NIVAC series, *Scot McKnight* (1996, £13.99/$22.99) does engage in exegesis before moving on to "bridging" and "contemporary significance." On *Simon J. Kistemaker*, see notes at §1.4.

Before Achtemier, the standard work on the Greek text was that of *E. G. Selwyn* (Macmillan 1946, op). This is one of the monumental pieces of industry that characterized the earlier Macmillan series. Most later commentaries have depended heavily on Selwyn. Hard on its heels came the work by *F. W. Beare* (1947, op), who rejects Petrine authorship and argues for a late date. The book is nevertheless full of exegetical insight. In the third edition (1970, op), Beare's commentary shows more dependence on Continental emphases on the putative liturgical origins of the epistle. Older works on the Greek text, including *C. A. Bigg* (ICC; 1902, op/$79.95), have been superseded. *J. Moffatt* (see under James) is concise and penetrating, primarily with respect to the actual situation of the original readers, but his work is now badly dated.

J. N. D. Kelly (BNTC/HNTC, on Peter and Jude; 1969, £19.99/reprint, Baker 1996, $29.95 hb) is very useful. It is thoughtful and sensitive in elucidating the thought of the epistles and brings out connections between 1 and 2 Peter. *Ernest Best* (NCB; 1982, op) is also a good commentary but not better than Kelly or Davids, let alone Michaels or Jobes. *C. E. B. Cranfield* (TBC with 2 Peter and Jude; 1960, op) is fresh and almost always useful but too brief to displace the larger works. The commentary by *D. Edmond Hiebert* (/Moody 1992, £13.50/op), like all of his commentaries, is gentle, cautious, and pious (in the best sense), but essentially a distillation of older work. *A. M. Hunter's* commentary in IB 12 (1957, op) is also useful. *A. M. Stibbs* (TNTC; 1959, op) is full of practical insights but has now been replaced by *Wayne Grudem* (1988, £9.99/$14.00). This is an independent exegesis—it interacts with little of the secondary literature—always worth consulting. Scholars and preachers alike will find the lengthy appendix on the "spirits in prison" passage (whether one agrees with it or not) to warrant the price of the book. *Donald Senior* on the Petrine epistles (NTM; 1980, £1.00/$6.95 pb) is clearly written but brief and unremarkable, but it has now been displaced by Senior's SP commentary (see above). The entry by *Edwin A. Blum* (EBC 12; see Morris on Hebrews) is slight.

It is no longer common to write commentaries on both 1 and 2 Peter in one volume (2 Peter and Jude are the more common collation), but *Fred B. Craddock* takes the older route and adds Jude in the WBComp volume (/1995, $19.95). His work is stronger on homiletic implications than on exegesis. The NIBC volume on 1 and 2 Peter by *Norman Hillyer* (1992, £6.99/$14.95) is sane and sensible.

The rise of sociological approaches to the NT is nowhere more clearly in evidence than in the modern study of 1 Peter. The commentary that generated not a little of this discussion is the German work by *Leonhard Goppelt* (MeyerK; 1978), which Eerdmans has brought out in English (/1993, op/$40.00). Goppelt's work is competent and detailed, and apart from spurring sociological approaches, it is rich in making links both to the Dead Sea Scrolls and to the Old Testament. In English the study that has precipitated sociological approaches to 1 Peter is that of John H. Elliott, *A Home for the Homeless* (1981, op). Though at many points it is suggestive, the thesis is overdone, and there are too few controls applied to the selection of sociological models. But treated with reserve, the approach has some value. Access to patristic comments is available from *Gerald Bray* (see ACCS entry on James).

The older four-volume devotional work by *Robert Leighton* (op) is worth skimming if you can read fast, but it is extraordinarily long for so short an epistle. The expository discourses of *John Brown* have been reprinted at various times. At the moment, the only one in print, so far as I know, is his *2 Peter Chapter 1: Parting Counsels* (BoT 1980, op/$12.95). *Gordon H. Clark* on the Petrine epistles (1980, op) can be thoughtful, sometimes frustrating, almost never humble, but occasionally a useful supplement to the standard works.

Popular commentaries abound. The best by far is the BST entry by *Edmund P. Clowney* (1994, £9.99/1989, $15.00). Perhaps I should mention three others: *Jay E. Adams* (1979, op); *Paul A. Cedar* (CC; see above on James); and *D. Stuart Briscoe* (/Harold Shaw 1993, /$8.99). *John Lillie*'s lectures on the Petrine epistles were reprinted by Klock and Klock in 1978, but they are again out of print. The commentary by *Martin Luther* on the epistles of Peter and Jude has been reprinted (/Kregel 1990, $13.99 pb).

3.19 2 Peter and Jude

Except in one or two instances, I shall not mention commentaries already discussed under James or 1 Peter, of which there are many (see especially Kelly, Cranfield, Moffatt, Reicke, Sidebottom, Hillyer, and Bigg).

By far the best work on 2 Peter and Jude is the exhaustive commentary by *Richard J. Bauckham* (WBC; 1983, £19.99/$39.99). There is no relevant literature up to his time that Bauckham has not considered, and he here puts to good use his knowledge of second temple Judaism and some of the more recent Gnostic finds. Why he concluded that 2 Peter is pseudonymous is still not clear to me: his evidence does not strike me as very convincing (see the brief but penetrating critique in the appendix of Grudem on 1 Peter). But this point should not put anyone off using what will be the standard in the field for decades to come. The contribution by *Jerome H. Neyrey* (/AB; 1993, $28.00) cannot compare with it. In any case, Neyrey's reconstruction of the settings of these epistles, though entertaining, is too speculative to be very useful to the serious preacher. Methodologically, he combines historical exegesis with approaches grounded in cultural anthropology, social science, and ancient rhetoric. This sometimes yields thought-provoking insight; more commonly, it builds castles out of thin air. His forays are so un-self-critical and so dogmatic that the commentary becomes an exercise in frustration. The contribution of *Steve J. Kraftchick*, on 2 Peter and Jude (/ANTC; 2002, $20.00), is far more useful to the preacher. Because he begins with exegesis, the NIVAC volume by *Douglas J. Moo* (1996, £24.99/$22.99) is worth reading. Don't overlook the FoB commentary by *Paul Gardner* (1998, £7.99/$14.99), certainly one of the stronger entries in that rather light series. The contribution by *Edland Waltner and J. Daryl Charles*, on 1 and 2 Peter and Jude (BCBC; 1999, $24.99), is so much akin to the corresponding updated commentaries by *J. Daryl Charles* in the new EBC (vol. 13; see above on Hebrews) that it is not worth using both.

A brief but admirable treatment of these two short epistles is found in *E. M. B. Green* (TNTC; 1968, rev. ed., 1987, op/$14.00). The Helps for Translators volume by *Daniel C. Arichea* (/UBS 1993, $22.99) is good but of course not rich in theology. The brief volume by *Jonathan Knight* is of course not strictly a commentary (NTG; 1995, £9.99/). It manages to be technically competent yet out of sympathy with the text being analyzed. The BST contribution, always of use to the preacher, is by *R. C. Lucas* and *Christopher Green* (1995, £9.99/$15.00). On the Greek text, although *J. B. Mayor*'s massive commentary has often been reprinted (most recently by /Baker 1979), it is again out of print. The work of *D. Edmond Hiebert* (/Bob Jones University Press 1989, $24.95) works reverently through the text but adds nothing of substance to Bauckham. The work of *Thomas Manton* on Jude has been reprinted by several companies: Kregel (/1988, £7.95 pb/$20.99 hb or $14.99 pb); Crossway (1999, £9.99 pb/$15.99 pb); and BoT (1989, £8.95 hb/1990, $24.99 hb).

3.20 Johannine Epistles

There are now four major commentaries in English (though two are translations from German) that are very full indeed—almost too full for some preachers who perhaps devote too little time to sermon preparation. The pastor will have to learn what sections to skim and what sections to read with minute care. The first is by *Raymond E. Brown* (/AB; 1983, op/1982, $55.00 hb)—a mammoth book that complements the author's two-volume commentary on John. Brown has changed his position somewhat since writing his volumes on the Fourth Gospel. He is far more certain that he can delineate the history of the Johannine community (cf. his *The Community of the Beloved Disciple*) than he used to be, and he is less certain that the writer of the Johannine epistles (whom he does not take to be the author of the Fourth Gospel) is a faithful interpreter of the Fourth Gospel. To put the matter another way, he is far more generous with the opponents John confronts in the epistles than seems warranted by the actual evidence. What is distinctive (and frankly unbelievable) in his exegesis of these epistles is that *everything* in 1 John is understood to have *specific* reference to the Fourth Gospel and its (mis)interpretation by the opponents. Nevertheless, the exegetical comments are often incisive, the bibliography invaluable (though now somewhat dated). The second major work is by *Stephen S. Smalley* (/ WBC; 1984, £19.99/$39.99). The bibliography is as good, and Smalley is at his best when he is summarizing and interacting with the positions of others. This work is a little more conservative than that of Brown (though I do not find Smalley's reconstruction of the setting very believable, with some opponents denying that Jesus is truly God and others denying that he is truly human). The comments themselves are not as incisive as those of Brown. Better than either is the ET of *Rudolf Schnackenburg* (Crossroad 1992, £35.00/$39.50), a moderately conservative Catholic scholar of the very first rank. The reasoning is constantly exegetical, historical, and theological. The ET of *Georg Strecker* (Hermeneia; 1996, £29.99 pb/$51.00 hb) is technically stimulating but certainly not as useful for the student and preacher. Astonishingly, Strecker locates the *Sitz im Leben* in the middle of the second century, which of course puts him at odds with the standard dating of two crucial papyri. Many of Strecker's positions reflect a kind of updating of old-fashioned history-of-religions positions. The center of these epistles is not Christology or faith or love but polemics, and Strecker's own interest lies primarily in the delineation of historical-theological "tendencies." Having said that, the detailed exegesis, the rich footnotes, and the nineteen excurses provide a cornucopia of learning for the scholar and well-equipped pastor. Others will give it a miss.

Several other recent commentaries written on a smaller scale deserve notice. The recent commentary by *Colin Kruse* (Pillar; 2000, £14.99/$30.00) is very accessible and has a fresh independence to it: it works happily out of primary sources and does not get bogged down in too many details (though clearly the author is aware of them). *John Painter* (SP; 2002, £29.99/$39.95) is a full-scale commentary that manages to be painfully dry and theologically thin. *Kenneth Grayston* (NCB; 1984, op) is too brief to be a first choice but is of some value because of its provocative positions (e.g., Grayston thinks the Johannine epistles were written before the Fourth Gospel). Of much more value to the preacher is *I. Howard Marshall* (NIC; rev. ed., 1995, £18.99/$32.00). The book is simply written and ably brings together a good deal of previous scholarship without getting bogged down in minutiae. In my view Marshall's theological commitments, in line with his book *Kept by the Power of God*, determine the exegesis here and there, but this is a very good commentary. The ACNT contribution by *Robert Kysar* (1986, £10.99/$17.25) is workmanlike and competent but not nearly as full. On *Simon J. Kistemaker*, see comments at §1.4. The NIBC commentary by *Thomas Floyd Johnson* (1995, £11.99/1993, $14.95) is not of the first rank. *David K. Rensberger* (/ANTC; 1997, $20.00) writes well. On many fronts he is a popularizer of the opinions of Raymond Brown. *D. Moody Smith* in the Interpretation series (1991, £14.99/$24.95) is too brief to belong to the first rank, but everywhere the positions adopted are carefully negotiated. The IVPNTC contribution by *Marianne Meye Thompson* (1992, £9.99/$16.00) is competent, sensible, and well written but somehow seems distant from John's passionate intensity. The NIVAC volume by *Gary M. Burge* (/1996, $22.99) is sensible, in some ways a breezy American counterpart to John Stott's TNTC volume (see below). The literary and theological commentary of *Charles H. Talbert* (Crossroad 1992, £15.00/$23.95) covers both the Fourth Gospel and the Johannine Epistles and is too slender on the latter to be very significant. Do not overlook the access to patristic comments in *Gerald Bray* (ACCS; above on James).

One of the most useful conservative commentaries on these epistles, so far as the preacher is concerned, is still that of *J. R. W. Stott* (TNTC; rev. ed.; 1988, £9.99/$14.00). It is packed with both exegetical comments and thoughtful application, and was the best in the old TNTC series. It is good to see it revised and holding its own in the new TNTC. *C. H. Dodd* (Moffatt; 1946, op) is highly praised by almost everyone, but I find it difficult to see why. The quality of his prose is superb, but he is so bound to his old-fashioned liberal tradition that on point after point he is wildly out of sympathy with the text. He insists, for instance, that John's quick definition "sin is lawlessness" is shallow, that 2 John must be condemned for its "fierce intolerance," and so forth. The Epworth commentary by *William R. Loader* (1992, £6.95/) is brief and innocuous. The Welwyn commentary by *Peter Barnes* (Evangelical Press 1998, £6.95/) is full of interesting quotes and the like, but it really is not in any sense a responsible exegesis of the Johannine Epistles. The commentary by *Tom Thatcher* in the new edition of EBC (vol. 13; 2006; see on Hebrews) is a cautious piece.

Two older commentaries retain some importance. *B. F. Westcott* on the Greek text has been periodically reprinted but is now out of print; *A. E. Brooke* (ICC; 1912, £28.95/$79.95) is still available. The latter was a standard in its day, but the best of its notes and comments have been picked up by the more recent works. *J. L. Houlden* (BNTC/HNTC; rev. ed.; 1994, £19.99 pb/op) is valuable, though in some ways Stott is still to be preferred. The Hermeneia series has been guilty of very bad judgment in some of its entries, and its initial choice in this case was one of them: *Rudolf Bultmann*'s ET (1973, now mercifully op) is so brief and so concerned with improbable source criticism that its remaining exegetical comments were never worth the price. Mercifully, it has now been replaced by the Strecker volume (above). *Gordon H. Clark*, on 1 John alone (Presbyterian & Reformed 1992, $10.95), is better on these epistles than on some others, but he shapes quite a bit of his argument against Bultmann, and on these epistles I doubt if Bultmann is influential enough to be worth the trouble.

Two important studies—sane, cautious, and insightful—are by Judith Lieu: *The Second and Third Epistles of John: History and Background*

(T&T Clark 1986, op/$33.95 pb) and *The Theology of the Johannine Epistles* (NTT; CUP 1991, £40.00 hb or £14.99 pb/$55.00 hb or $20.99 pb). One does not have to agree with all her positions to mine these books for a great deal of thoughtful evaluation. Akin to the work by Parsons and Culy on Acts (see above) is a slender book by Martin M. Culy, *I, II, III John: A Handbook on the Greek Text* (Baylor University Press 2004, £14.50/$19.95)—not really a commentary but just what the subtitle says. Similarly, see S. M. Baugh, *A First John Reader: Intermediate Greek Reading Notes and Grammar* (/Presbyterian & Reformed 1999, $18.99).

The recent commentary by *Donald W. Burdick* (/Moody 1985, op) is not to be overlooked, although not always to be trusted. Almost five hundred pages in length, it attempts to offer exegesis of the Greek text, theological comment, present-day application, and some comments on structure. But beware: its approach to Greek somehow manages to be simultaneously painstaking and mechanical, partly because the work is linguistically uninformed. The style is a bit stodgy, but at least the author is interested in theological questions (though he is perhaps too little interested in the history that has provoked them). This work is not to be confused with his purely popular commentary on these epistles (/Moody 1970, £3.75 pb/$9.99 pb). Two older classics are Robert Law, *The Tests of Life* (regrettably op), and George B. Findlay, *Studies in John's Epistles: Fellowship in the Life Eternal* (reprint, Kregel [1909] 1989, $17.99 pb). Both of these works are eminently quotable, but they have been culled by more recent writers, notably Stott. The little commentary by *F. F. Bruce* (rev. ed.; Eerdmans [1978] 1990, op/$10.00 pb) is a series of studies first published as articles in *The Witness* and is well worth reading. The essays that make up most of R. E. O. White's *An Open Letter to Evangelicals: A Devotional and Homiletical Commentary on the First Epistle of John* (op), though well written, is theologically tepid compared with 1 John itself, but the "Notes" on the text at the end of the book are excellent.

Popular works abound. Among the better ones are *J. W. Roberts* (/Abilene Christian University Press 1984, $12.95) and *R. Alan Culpepper* (KPG; 1985, op). In 1982, Klock and Klock reprinted the massive work (612 pp.) of *J. Morgan and S. Cox*, but it is again out of print. So also is *Alfred Plummer*—in any case not his finest hour.

3.21 Revelation

Of the writing of books on Revelation there is no end: most generations produce far too many. It is a little-known fact that the Puritans, for instance, produced far more commentaries on Revelation than on any other book, most of them eminently forgettable and mercifully forgotten. Something similar could be said about most periods of church history, including our own. But several excellent commentaries are available to compensate for a great deal of nonsense. One of the preacher's or student's first requirements, before plunging into the "application," is to find a couple of commentators who understand the nature and purpose of apocalyptic. In this respect, we might wisely turn to *G. B. Caird* (BNTC/HNTC; 1985, £19.99/1993, $24.95) or *G. R. Beasley-Murray* (NCB; 1981, op). Caird's commentary has now been replaced by *Ian Boxall* (announced for June 2006; I have not yet seen it). But Revelation also represents the prophetic tradition, and this is underlined by *Leon Morris* (TNTC; rev. ed.; 1987, £9.99/$14.00) and *George Ladd* (Eerdmans 1971, £9.99 pb/$18.00 pb). Perhaps the best single volume at a highly accessible level is that of *Robert H. Mounce* (NIC; rev. ed.; 1997, £27.99/$48.00)—a learned and well-written work that not only explains the text satisfactorily in most instances but also introduces the student to the best of the secondary literature. Not to be overlooked is the work of *J. P. Sweet*, listed with the Pelican series on the British side (1979, op) and now with TPINT on the American (1990, $25.00). Longer than most contributions to the Pelican series, this commentary is insightful at many points and includes an able discussion of the degree of persecution that did (or did not!) take place under Emperor Domitian. Other mid-level commentaries that are well worth reading include *Ben Witherington III* (NCBC; CUP 2003, £15.99/$21.99), a more rounded work than his typical "socio-rhetorical" commentaries; and *Craig S. Keener* (NIVAC; 2000, £17.99/$29.00).

For those with adequate training, however, more substantial works take pride of place. Four of these are on the Greek text. The commentary that best combines comprehensiveness with biblical fidelity is that of *G. K. Beale* (/NIGTC; 2000, $75.00). The prose is sometimes dense, and, inevitably (not least in a book like this!), readers will want to disagree with him from time to time—but there are few significant things that Beale has not thought deeply about. He is especially good in untangling how the Apocalypse incorporates Old Testament passages and themes. Even more massive than Beale's work is the three-volume set of *David E. Aune* (/WBC; 3 vols.; 1997–1998, $39.99 each). The handling of the Greek text, at the level of grammar, is often superb. The prose is accessible, the arguments often elegant. Aune frequently insists that more attention be paid to the Greco-Roman parallels than is done by those who fasten onto Jewish parallels and sources, and sometimes he makes a convincing case. He is very good at locating this book within the political and cultural matrix of its day. Yet I do not think that Aune is as good as Beale at coming to terms with the book's message with categories and priorities that the author himself would have recognized. Rather astonishingly, he opts for a complex source-critical approach to the Apocalypse. Surrounding questions are given such weight that the space devoted to thought-provoking exegesis of the document itself, on its own terms, is much less than the bulk of the commentary might lead one to expect. *Stephen S. Smalley* (SPCK 2005, £40.00 pb/IVP 2005, $65.00 hb) is a competent piece of work, less daunting than Beale and less tendentious than Aune. Finally, the commentary by *Grant R. Osborne* (/BECNT; 2002, $49.99) is especially good at laying out what the options are.

Not a commentary, but very important for coming to grips with the message of Revelation, is the book by Richard Bauckham, *The Climax of Prophecy: Studies on the Book of Revelation* (T&T Clark 1999, £30.00 pb/$46.95 pb). The SP contribution by *Wilfrid J. Harrington* (1993, £31.50/$34.95) is certainly responsible, but it simply isn't long enough to compare with more substantial volumes in the series or with a commentary like that of Mounce (above). The same thing must be said of the ET of *Jürgen Roloff* (Fortress 1993, /$28.50), the NIBC volume by *Robert W. Wall* (1995, £11.99 pb/$14.99), and the ANTC volume by *Leonard L. Thompson* (/1998, $22.00)—though the latter is nicely informed by extensive knowledge of first-century history and culture (see his monograph, below). The slender IVPNTC volume by *J. Ramsey Michaels* (/1997, $20.00) falls into the same camp, of course, but for its size and level it is elegantly written, packed with good things, and displays a good deal of independent judgment: one does not get the impression that Michaels is merely parroting what earlier commentaries have said. *Joseph L. Trafton* (/Smyth & Helwys 2005, $21.00) is undistinguished.

The commentary by *George Wesley Buchanan* (/MBC; 1993, $139.95) cannot compete with the longer volumes, of course; it interacts with only the more obvious secondary literature, the prose does not always flow well, the price is outrageous, and the transliterations are eccentric. Nevertheless, because of its focus on intertextuality, this commentary offers interesting observations on the use of antecedent Scripture in Revelation that are not found elsewhere. *Josephine Massyngberde Ford* (/AB; 1975, $39.95 hb or 1995, $32.50 pb) is entertaining, primarily because it is eccentric. John the Baptist, we are told, was responsible for most of Revelation—but perhaps that is not too surprising from a scholar who has argued that the Blessed Virgin penned Hebrews. Ford's background material, especially from Qumran, would have been invaluable, had more of her references been right: in one section I checked, fully one-third of the references were incorrect. The two volumes of *Robert L. Thomas* (/Moody, 2 vols.; 1992–95, $39.99 and $42.00 respectively) uphold, competently enough, an old-fashioned pre-tribulational premillennialism. Although it is again out of print, Austin Farrar's *The Rebirth of Images* enjoys good runs now and then. It too is idiosyncratic, its title betraying the key it offers to help readers interpret Revelation; but it is strangely powerful and evocative. Paul S. Minear, *I Saw a New Earth* (1968, op), draws on sound biblical scholarship to show the relevance of Revelation to the present day—though "present day" is becoming dated. More difficult to assess in brief compass is David Chilton, *The Days of Vengeance: An Exposition of the Book of Revelation* (/Dominion 1987, $24.95). The book is strongest where it brings together from larger, more technical commentaries something of the wealth of Old Testament allusions and shows their relevance to the interpretation of the Apocalypse. But Chilton ties his interpretation of the entire book to a dogmatic insistence that it was written before AD 70 and that its predictions are focused on the destruction of Jerusalem. Although there are some excellent theological links crafted in this book, the central setting and argument are so weak and open to criticism that I cannot recommend the work very warmly. The lengthy (18 pp.) "Publisher's Preface" by Gary North is so arrogant and condescending it is embarrassing: I earnestly hope Chilton found it so. The UBS Handbook by *Robert G. Bratcher* (/1993, $23.99) is one of the stronger entries in that series, but of course the series does not emphasize the theology of the book. The social-science commentary by *Bruce J. Malina* (Fortress 2000, £11.99/$20.00) adds little to the major commentaries already listed; it merely focuses attention on certain select phenomena in the text and in the historical background, and unwittingly distorts the power of the text. *Pablo Richard*'s slim volume (Orbis 1995, £11.99/$20.00) reads the Apocalypse as a support for liberation theology. Other slim introductions to the Apocalypse include *J. Knight* in the Readings series (SAP 1999, £55.00 hb or £15.95 pb/$120.00 hb or $26.50 pb)—outrageously priced—and *John M. Court* in the NTG series (1995, £12.99/$25.95).

The traditional conservative commentary for many pastors until fairly recently was that of W. Hendriksen, viz. *More Than Conquerors* ([1939] 1982, $14.99). In some circles this book has been assigned almost legendary value, but one must assume that the reason lies primarily in the combination of sober interpretation and evangelical fervor, all of it easily accessible, at a time when evangelicals were not producing much of worth on Revelation. It is now entirely eclipsed by more recent commentaries. In the same tradition, for instance, *Simon J. Kistemaker* (NTC; 2001, £29.99/$44.99) is far superior, and so, in briefer compass, is *Dennis E. Johnson* (/Presbyterian & Reformed 2001, $24.99)—though Johnson manages to include a few eccentricities. The Seventh Day Adventists now have a major champion in *Ranko Stefanovic* (/Andrews University Press 2002, $39.99); the believers' church tradition is well represented by *John R. Yeatts* (BCBC; 2003, £21.50/$29.99); and the

Restorationist movement by *Christopher A. Davis* (/CPNIVC; 2000, $32.99). *W. Barclay* (DSB; 2 vols.; St Andrew/Westminster 1976, £6.50 each/$29.00 hb each or $12.95 pb each) is still of some practical value. *Alan F. Johnson* (EBC 12; see Morris on Hebrews; sold separately in paperback, Zondervan 1996, £9.99/$16.99) has written the best commentary in this volume of EBC; moreover, he has updated it for the new EBC (vol. 13; see entry under Hebrews, above). *Ludwig van Hartingsveld* (Eerdmans 1986, op), translated from the Dutch, offers virtually no interaction with other views (a "must" for a useful commentary on a book like Revelation) and provides little grist for the modern expositor (despite the subtitle of this series: "Text and Interpretation: A Practical Commentary"). *Sean P. Kealy* (Glazier 1991, £12.50/Liturgical 1987, $17.95) offers in fairly short space a lot of clear, interpretative help at the historical level, but the author finally endorses so existentialist an interpretation that much of the good is vitiated. *Philip E. Hughes* (Pillar; 1990, op/$22.00) is too short to be anyone's first choice. It bodes well to replace Hendriksen. Although Hughes has many of the themes right, in my view he has the interpretation of not a few passages wrong. There is little interaction with other literature.

H. B. Swete on the Greek text has often been reprinted but is now again out of print. Swete is normally stodgy and often dull, but although he never shakes off his pedestrianism, in this commentary there is some really useful and thorough material that helps the reader to see the depth of the book. *M. Kiddle* (Moffatt; op) is simply too verbose: the sum of its fruitful comment hardly justifies the number of pages it occupies.

Three experts on Revelation toward the beginning of the century were *R. H. Charles* (ICC; 2 vols.; 1920, £59.95/$89.95 each), *Isbon T. Beckwith* (Macmillan; 1922, op), and, to a lesser extent, *W. Milligan* (EB; 1891, op). Charles in particular should not be overlooked, in view of the immense scholarship it represents. In one sense it has not been surpassed, but the preacher should not set too much hope on it, as the two volumes are very technical and only rarely practical. Beckwith is almost as good and more accessible to those who have a command of Greek. Milligan oscillates between the excellent and the disappointing. *James Moffatt* (EGT, 5 vols.; Eerdmans 1952, op) still repays study. *Martin*

Rist (IB; see §1.2.3 for details) claims to offer one or two completely original thoughts, but there is no dearth of scholars who claim to do this on the book of Revelation.

Not a commentary but a stimulating collection of essays is found in Elisabeth Schüssler Fiorenza, *The Book of Revelation: Justice and Judgment* (Fortress 1984, £12.99 pb/$21.00 pb), who follows Käsemann in understanding apocalyptic in terms of power. After being out of print for some years, Colin J. Hemer, *The Letters to the Seven Churches of Asia*, is once again available (/Eerdmans 2000, $32.00). It is by far the most detailed and even-handed study of Revelation 2–3, steeped in suggestive details—though of course the preacher will have to draw the appropriate applications. Leonard L. Thompson, *The Book of Revelation: Apocalypse and Empire* (OUP 1997, £17.00/1996, $27.50 pb), is a series of useful essays tracing many of Revelation's themes against the background of the social history and politics of the period and debunking not a few popular but clearly erroneous assumptions. The volume by *Christopher Rowland* in BBC (2003, $31.95 pb) focuses on the reception of the book—no small matter for a book like the Apocalypse. The massive seventeenth-century commentary by *James Durham* has been reprinted (Old Paths [1658] 2000, $69.96). One should not overlook the access to patristic comments provided by *Walter C. Weinrich* (/ACCS; 2005, $40.00).

There is no end of shorter or lighter commentaries. The standard popular dispensational commentary today is probably still that of *John F. Walvoord* (/Moody 1995, £11.25/1989 [originally 1966], $19.95). *Elisabeth Schüssler Fiorenza* (/ProcC; 1991, $16.00) and *James L. Blevins* (KPG; 1984, op) are both so brief that they scarcely deserve a quick skim. *Charles H. Giblin* (Liturgical 1991, £15.50/$16.95) is designed for laypeople and is organized around the theme of "God's holy war of liberation." *Kendall H. Easley* (/HNTC; Broadman & Holman 1998, $19.99) is equally suited to lay use. *Christopher Rowland* enjoys a vast knowledge of apocalyptic literature, and that knowledge is put to good use within the severe restraints of the Epworth series (Epworth 1994, £9.99/TPI 1993, $13.50)—which is not to be confused with his BBC volume (see above). At the very popular level (suitable for distribution among laypeople while you expound the text week by week) is the little book by Richard Bewes, *The Lamb Wins!* (Christian Focus 2000, £5.99/). Innovative in its design is the work edited by Steve Gregg, *Revelation: Four Views. A Parallel Commentary* (/Thomas Nelson 1997, $32.99). *M. Eugene Boring* in the Interpretation series (Westminster John Knox 1989, £17.99/$29.95) has much more substance, though Boring sometimes tries to import his views on the prophetic words of the exalted Jesus into the text. William Still, *A Vision of Glory: An Exposition of the Book of Revelation* (Nicholas Gray 1987, op), is a slim volume that will help some laypeople. In fact there are scores and scores of slim or popular expositions, some of them reliable but too thin to be useful to the preacher, many of them merely fanciful. One of the best is Vern Poythress, *The Returning King: A Guide to the Book of Revelation* (Presbyterian & Reformed 2000, $14.99 pb). In this book Poythress wears his learning lightly, but it is apparent that he has read widely and thought through the biblical text. Among other responsible popular treatments, however much one might want to disagree with this or that detail, is the BST volume by Michael Wilcock, *I Saw Heaven Opened: The Message of Revelation* (1984, £9.99/1988, $15.00). One should not overlook the popularization Robert H. Mounce has provided of his NIC commentary (see above) in *What Are We Waiting For? A Commentary on Revelation* (Eerdmans 1992, op). This may give the preacher some practical hints, but it should not be used without careful reading of the NIC volume. The book by Arthur Wainwright, *Mysterious Apocalypse: Interpreting the Book of Revelation* (Abingdon 1994; reprint, Wipf & Stock 2001, $29.00), is rather less a commentary and more a history of the interpretation of the book of Revelation. For a more technical history, one should turn to Gerhard Maier, *Die Johannesoffenbarung und die Kirche* (WUNT 25; Mohr Siebeck 1981, op).

4

SOME "BEST BUYS"

This brief list does not pretend to identify which is the "best" commentary on every New Testament book: the opening pages of this *Survey* have already made it clear that what is "best" can vary from reader to reader and depends in any case on what kind of information a particular reader is looking for—quite apart from the theological orientation of particular commentaries. The following rather subjective list identifies commentaries that are a good value for the money for the theological student or well-trained preacher who is interested in understanding the Scriptures and who is willing to read commentaries critically.

Matthew	W. D. Davies & D. C. Allison or J. Nolland for advanced students; C. Keener; Craig Blomberg
Mark	R. T. France for advanced students; J. Brooks
Luke	D. Bock or Jon Nolland for advanced students; W. L. Leifeld or L. T. Johnson
John	C. Keener for advanced students; H. Ridderbos; A. J. Köstenberger
Acts	C. K. Barrett for advanced students; B. Witherington III; I. H. Marshall

Romans	D. J. Moo in NIC; T. Schreiner; C. E. B. Cranfield for advanced students; A. Nygren
1 Corinthians	A. Thiselton; G. D. Fee; D. Garland
2 Corinthians	M. J. Harris; D. E. Garland
Galatians	F. F. Bruce; R. N. Longenecker
Ephesians	P. T. O'Brien; H. W. Hoehner; A. T. Lincoln
Philippians	P. T. O'Brien; M. Silva; G. D. Fee; M. Bockmuehl
Colossians/Philemon	P. T. O'Brien; J. D. G. Dunn
Thessalonians	C. A. Wanamaker; G. Green
Pastorals	I. H. Marshall; W. D. Mounce; L. T. Johnson; J. D. Quinn and W. C. Wacker; P. Towner
Hebrews	P. Ellingworth; W. Lane; for historical perspective, P. Hughes
James	P. H. Davids in NIGTC or NIBC; D. J. Moo in Pillar; L. T. Johnson
1 Peter	P. J. Achtemeier, with some discretion; K. Jobes or P. H. Davids; I. Howard Marshall
2 Peter and Jude	R. Bauckham
Johannine Epistles	R. Schnackenburg for advanced students; C. Kruce; I. H. Marshall; J. R. W. Stott
Revelation	G. K. Beale; R. H. Mounce; for background in the Greco-Roman world, D. E. Aune

NAME INDEX